HENRY DESPENSER THE FIGHTING BISHOP

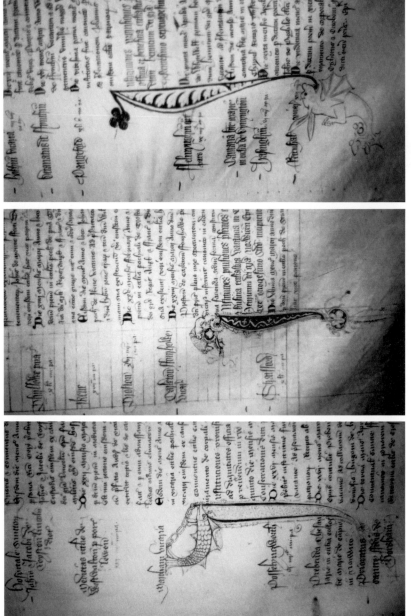

Three drawings from the Bishop's Register by Master William Ferriby

HENRY DESPENSER
THE
FIGHTING BISHOP

⤭⤬

Richard Allington-Smith

Canon Emeritus of Norwich Cathedral

Larks Press

Published by the Larks Press
Ordnance Farmhouse, Guist Bottom
Dereham, Norfolk NR20 5PF
01328 829207
email: Larks.Press@btinternet.com
website: www.booksatlarkspress.co.uk

Printed by the Lanceni Press
Garrood Drive, Fakenham
01328 851578

British Library Cataloguing-in-Publication Data
A catalogue record for this book is available
from the British Library

ISBN 1 904006 16 7

Foreword

A number of people have helped me to produce this book, and I am anxious to thank them all.

The original idea came, indirectly, from Bishop Maurice Wood, formerly of Norwich. Although I have never been a member of the University of East Anglia, three of its historians have given me much assistance. I refer to Dr Diana Wood, Professor Christopher Harper-Bill and the late Dr Roger Virgoe. I am also indebted to the officials of the Norfolk Record Office, who have Bishop Henry's voluminous Register in their care. Several trips to the Cambridge University Library have profited from the care and courtesy of the members of its staff.

I am most grateful to Mrs Susan Yaxley, who has seen the manuscript through the press, and to Malcolm Raymer, a fellow-member of the Rotary Club of Norwich, who placed his skills as a photographer at my disposal.

But most of all I thank my wife Pat for her continued encouragement and forbearance. It is to her that I dedicate this book.

Richard Allington-Smith

Contents

—※◆※—

Illustrations

Family Tree of Henry Despenser

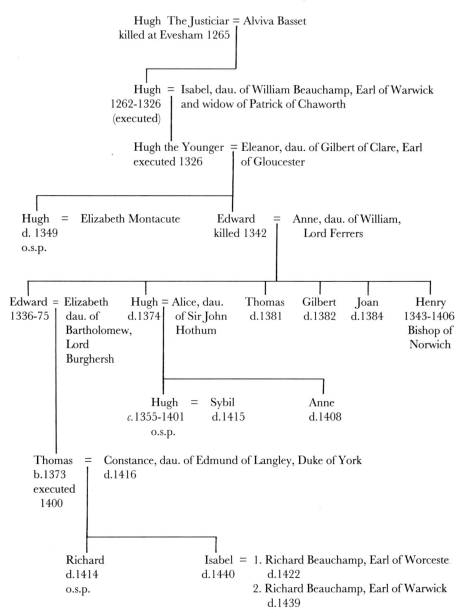

Hugh The Justiciar = Alviva Basset
killed at Evesham 1265

Hugh = Isabel, dau. of William Beauchamp, Earl of Warwick
1262-1326 and widow of Patrick of Chaworth
(executed)

Hugh the Younger = Eleanor, dau. of Gilbert of Clare, Earl
executed 1326 of Gloucester

Hugh = Elizabeth Montacute   Edward = Anne, dau. of William,
d. 1349   killed 1342   Lord Ferrers
o.s.p.

Edward = Elizabeth   Hugh = Alice, dau.   Thomas   Gilbert   Joan   Henry
1336-75   dau. of   d.1374   of Sir John   d.1381   d.1382   d.1384   1343-1406
        Bartholomew,   Hothum   Bishop of
        Lord   Norwich
        Burghersh

Hugh = Sybil   Anne
c.1355-1401   d.1415   d.1408
o.s.p.

Thomas = Constance, dau. of Edmund of Langley, Duke of York
b.1373   d.1416
executed
1400

Richard   Isabel = 1. Richard Beauchamp, Earl of Worceste:
d.1414   d.1440   d.1422
o.s.p.   2. Richard Beauchamp, Earl of Warwick
                                        d.1439

Note: The order of birth of the six children of Edward Despenser (d.1342) is uncertain

1. Knight's Move to Bishop 1343-1370

The family of Despenser, or Le Despenser, originated before the Norman Conquest from the lords of Gommiecourt in the county of Artois, in north-eastern France.[1] After the Conquest, as their name implies, they were dispensers of wine, or wine-stewards, though not to the king himself. That honour *(Dispensator Regis)* was in the hands of another family of the same name but quite unrelated. Our Despensers provided wine for the Earls of Chester, or possibly the Lacy family when they held the office of Constable of that city.[2]

The Despensers emerged into prominence with the first Hugh (a favourite family name), who was an associate of Simon de Montfort and Justiciar of England. He was killed with Simon at the battle of Evesham in 1265, an event commemorated by a memorial window in the church of St Laurence where the Despenser arms are prominently displayed.

By contrast the second and third Hughs, usually known as the Elder and the Younger, exercised a malign influence as favourites of King Edward II. Both were barbarously executed in 1326. The younger Hugh had, however, married Eleanor de Clare, sister and heiress of Gilbert de Clare, last of his line, who was killed at Bannockburn in 1314. She brought with her part of the De Clare inheritance and with it royal blood, for her mother Joan of Acre was the daughter of King Edward I. Thus, in the fullness of time, Henry Despenser, Bishop of Norwich, could claim kinship with Edward III, Richard II and Henry IV, a fact frequently acknowledged in official documents.[3]

With the evil deeds of the two Despensers, Elder and Younger, fresh in his mind, Edward III might have been excused had he regarded their descendants with coolness if not with animosity. He did neither. Following the biblical precept,[4] he treated the younger Hugh's sons well and received in return loyalty and faithful service, though the de Clare earldom of Gloucester is heard of no more until the final years of the century.

The next Hugh (Hugh the Younger's eldest son) played a distinguished part in the opening phases of the Hundred Years War. He fought at Sluys in 1340 and at Crécy in 1346, when his retinue comprised 2 knights banneret, 40 knights bachelor, 86 esquires and 105 archers. He is also credited with the capture of the town of Crotoy on 24 August, 1346. Eight years earlier he had been summoned to Parliament as Lord Le Despenser. When he died without issue, possibly of the Black Death, Edward III owed him £2,770.[5] His effigy, the first of the great line of Tewkesbury monuments, lies serenely with that of his wife Elizabeth Montacute, under a magnificent stone canopy in the north

1

ambulatory of the abbey church. He is clad in an early form of the camail and jupon armour, mixed mail and plate, so familiar to us through other monuments and brasses of the period. Nearby is the tomb of Sir Guy de Brien, Elizabeth's second husband, a renowned soldier and man of affairs, who had outlived her by over thirty years when he died in 1390.

Sir Edward Despenser, Hugh's younger brother, has no monument at Tewkesbury. He married Anne, daughter of William, Lord Ferrers of Groby, possibly in 1334. The union was destined to last for only eight years, as Edward was killed at the siege of Vannes in 1342.[6] But it was astonishingly fruitful. No fewer than six children were born, five boys and a girl.[7] One hopes that there were twins among them; in any case Anne's sorrow at her bereavement was probably tempered by freedom from incessant child-bearing. With the primitive obstetrics of that time this would almost certainly have hastened her own demise.

How do we catalogue and classify this numerous progeny? There are in fact only two fixed points. The eldest son, we know, was Edward, for he inherited the title of Lord Le Despenser from his uncle and was 39 years of age when he died in 1375. Henry, equally certainly, was the youngest. The papal dispensation granting him the see of Norwich, dated 3 April, 1370, states that he is in his twenty-seventh year.[8] This, taken in conjunction with his father's death in 1342, suggests that he was born after that death took place, possibly in the first half of 1343.

Of all Henry's siblings his eldest brother Edward exerted the greatest influence, and that influence appears to have been entirely good and positive. Edward was in fact one of the most renowned and chivalrous knights of his day. Born and baptised at Essendine in Rutland on 24 March, 1336, he began his military career on the expedition that culminated in the battle of Poitiers in 1356. Summoned to Parliament as Lord Le Despenser in 1357, he was created Knight of the Garter in 1361 and acted as Constable of the English army during John of Gaunt's unsuccessful invasion of France in 1373. Earlier, he had fought with distinction in the papal army in Italy, and was to finish his military career in Brittany. Nor were his gifts confined to military affairs. His courtesy and charm of manner were such that, according to the great ladies of the time, no feast could be perfect unless he was there. Commenting on his death, early even for those times, Froissart, who knew him well, says that he was 'deeply mourned by all his friends. He was a noble heart and a gallant knight, open-handed and chivalrous. May God have mercy on his soul'.[9]

Certainly the great chronicler's estimate is borne out from other sources. As the holder of the main family estates Edward was not unmindful of the needs of his less well-endowed younger brothers.[10] Henry too appears to have had

Edward's unfailing support; and he may well have gained his bishopric from the right word spoken at the right time into receptive papal ears.

So it is not unfitting that Edward Despenser should have at Tewkesbury a monument unlike any other to be found in England. Above his chantry chapel, itself a thing of great beauty, his armoured effigy kneels below an elaborate canopy, eyes gazing towards the high altar and gauntletted hands at prayer. The detail of this remarkable work is of the highest quality, as modern restoration and cleaning have revealed.[11]

What of the brothers and sister intermediate between Edward and Henry? Little can be said with any degree of precision, for although we know when they died, we are ignorant of the order in which they were born.

The 'Kneeling Knight', the monument to Edward Despenser in Tewkesbury Abbey

There is, however, some reason to believe that Sir Hugh (all the brothers became knights) was next in line after Edward. He died at Padua in Italy in early March, 1374, at which time his son and heir, yet another Hugh, was said to be eighteen years of age and more.[12] He married Alice, daughter of Sir John Hothum of Bonby in Lincolnshire. She died in October, 1379, when this same son was said to be 24 years of age, which might suggest that his father was born around 1336. Hugh's main properties (beside Bonby, brought in by his wife) were at Solihull in Warwickshire and Collyweston in Northamptonshire, a place well-known for the manufacture of stone roof-tiles.

The younger Hugh, Sir Hugh Despenser of Collyweston, died in October, 1401. He then occupied the important post of tutor to Prince Henry, the future Henry V, and it speaks volumes for his abilities and trustworthiness that he was so honoured in spite of the hostile attitude of his uncle Bishop Henry and his cousin Lord Thomas Despenser towards the House of Lancaster. Sir Hugh the younger had no heir by his wife Sybil (d. 1415), and neither did his sister Anne (d. 1408), to whom the property passed, from her unhappy union with Sir Edward Botyler (d. 1412).

To judge from the place of his premature death Edward and Henry Despenser had persuaded their brother Hugh the elder to follow their example and become involved in the Italian wars.[13] Another brother, Thomas, was also a knight in more than name. In the same unsuccessful French expedition of 1373, in which his brother Edward was Constable of the army, he was taken prisoner in a skirmish at Ouchy-les-Soissons, a misfortune which no doubt required the payment of a substantial ransom.[14] Perhaps the ever-generous Edward helped here as well, as he had already done with property. Nevertheless Thomas held two-thirds of the manor of Mapledurwell in Hampshire as tenant-in-chief of the king; and he was closely involved, with his mother, in the administration of part of the important manor of Burghley, just outside Stamford. This, the gift of Edward III, was later to be the seat of Elizabeth I's Secretary of State, William Cecil, Lord Burghley. Complex legal arrangements concerning Burghley involved, at one time or another, most of the members of the family, including Sir Philip Le Despenser, who belonged to the other Despenser family mentioned earlier.[15] Like his brother Hugh, Thomas was a considerable person in the East Midlands when he died unmarried in February, 1381.[16] His property therefore passed to the young son of Edward Despenser, Thomas, who was to lose it through his attainder and death in 1400.

Perhaps it was the need to oversee affairs at Burghley after Thomas' death that drew Bishop Henry so far away from his diocese at the time of the Peasants' Revolt in June, 1381.

This leaves the final brother, Gilbert. As early as 1368 he received a grant of 40 marks per annum at the Exchequer for life until further order.[17] As to landed property he held the manor of Thorley in the Isle of Wight,[18] together with the manor of La Brodetoune in or near Wootton Basset in Wiltshire. The latter, devised to him for life by his brother Hugh, was charged with a yearly pension of 10 marks in favour of the abbess and convent of Shaftesbury during the life of Joan Le Despenser their sister, a nun of that house.[19] Clearly the family was anxious that this lady should fulfil her vocation in the best possible place, for Shaftesbury was a most prestigious nunnery for daughters of the aristocracy. Whether it really was a vocation must remain uncertain; poor Joan had no future as an heiress with so many brothers. Her death occurred in 1384, two years after that of Gilbert, who was also unmarried.[20] This meant that by far the greater part of the family wealth was eventually concentrated in the hands of Edward's son Thomas. Born in 1373 he did not take after his gallant and

4

honourable father, but seems to have had more in common with the two ill-fated Hughs of the first quarter of the century. High in favour with Richard II he received the long-coveted earldom of Gloucester when the latter distributed honours and promotions wholesale in 1397. But neither it nor he lasted long after the usurpation of Henry IV. Soon after reverting to Lord Despenser he became involved in the rebellion of 1400, and avoided the inevitable execution for treason only by being unceremoniously lynched by the people of Bristol.[21] His young son, Richard, succeeded him, but only to his attainder.[22] After Richard died without heirs in 1414 the Despenser inheritance passed through his sister Isabel (d. 1440), first to Richard Beauchamp, Earl of Worcester (d. 1422) and then to his namesake and her second husband the great Earl of Warwick (d. 1439). Through the latter's daughter Anne it then went to the even more famous Richard Neville, also Earl of Warwick, 'the Kingmaker' (d. 1471), and thence, via his daughters Isabella (d. 1476) and Anne (d. 1484), it moved to the Yorkist Plantagenets George, Duke of Clarence (d. 1478) and King Richard III (d. 1485). But these events are well beyond the scope of this enquiry.

Mention of the Yorkists, however, recalls the fact that in 1461, when Edward IV assumed the throne after the battle of Towton, two of those done to death and attainted in 1400 were rehabilitated in Parliament and the attainders reversed. One of them was Lord Thomas Despenser, and in this way, long after their day was done, the clan to which he had added little lustre was enrolled as honorary supporter of the new dynasty. The entry announcing the rehabilitation is so colourful that it defies relegation to the notes attached to this chapter. It is recited that:

> 'certeyn persones of evill riotous and cedicious disposicion, joyned in rumour and rebellious novelryes, tirannyously murdred with grete cruelte and horrible violence in an outerageous hedy fury the right noble and werthy lordes John Montague late erle of Salesbury and Thomas late Lorde le Despenser.'[23]

Having reviewed his family we must now concentrate on Henry Despenser himself. Being the youngest of five brothers the best arena for his future activities was probably thought to be the Church. He was in good company, for William Courtenay and Thomas Arundel, both future Archbishops of Canterbury, were contemporaries and shared the same background. Experience, however, shows that such schemes sometimes run up against a human element which is unwilling to conform.

Here an element of imagination is required. Henry Despenser, a fatherless boy, found himself growing up in a family that had exchanged its somewhat

5

dubious past for a decidedly glamorous present through the activities of his eldest brother Edward, not to mention his father Edward who had died before the walls of Vannes before his son had even entered the world. Nor must we forget his uncle Hugh, who lived long enough to impress himself to some extent on a lively and enthusiastic little boy, and Sir Guy de Brien, who took his place as an honorary uncle.

But the predominant influence seems to have been that of Edward, the renowned 'kneeling knight' of Tewkesbury, of whom Froissart speaks with such enthusiasm and genuine feeling. Whereas his younger brothers held comparatively modest estates, adequate to support their degree of knighthood, Edward held lands all over England and even, by right of his wife, in Ireland.[24] Nevertheless his power base (and a formidable one it was) is to be found in the West Country and in South Wales. Beside important holdings in Gloucestershire at Fairford, Chipping Sodbury and Tewkesbury itself,[25] he held the great Marcher lordship of Glamorgan with its castles of Cardiff, Cærphilly, Lantrissen (?Llantrissant), Talvan, Kenfeg and Neath. To this, through the inheritance of Elizabeth his wife, daughter of Bartholomew, Lord Burghersh, he had added the castle and a moiety of the lordship of Ewyas, not far from the Welsh border in Herefordshire. Other assets (interesting in view of the later history of South Wales) included a coal mine at Senghenydd, destined to be the scene of a terrible mining disaster in 1913, the worst Wales has ever experienced.

We can therefore envisage Henry growing up in an atmosphere of castles, men-at-arms, archers and tales of warlike accomplishments, the whole presided over by his charismatic elder brother Edward, who was visited from time to time by other celebrated lords and knights. For this was very much the age of chivalry. Its tenets and aspirations were taken most seriously by knights of the time like Sir John Chandos and others who appear in the pages of Froissart. Pre-eminent among them was the Black Prince himself. Of course not all knights and esquires lived up to these standards, as Henry was to find to his cost at the time of the Peasants' Revolt, and even more during his crusade to Flanders in 1383. For some, as present-day cynicism might suggest, chivalry was no more than a veneer in a thoroughly brutal world, but such as Edward Despenser seem to have been entirely sincere in their view of the solemn responsibilities of knighthood. What is more, the fourteenth century witnessed a revival of the crusading ideal that was undoubtedly genuine, though for many it was a pious aspiration unlikely to be realised in practice except, perhaps, in the company of the Teutonic Knights in Poland and the lands adjoining the Baltic Sea. Even so, Chaucer's Knight in the *Canterbury Tales* is depicted as both pious and widely travelled. Presumably the poet did not wish him to be regarded as exceptional.[26]

6

To what extent a boy destined for the Church was expected or encouraged to join the rigorous training that led to knighthood we have no means of telling. But given Henry's adventurous and unconventional disposition, so frequently displayed in later years, one suspects that any attempt to deny him these activities would not have been received at all well. Often, of course, boys of gentle birth were boarded out with another noble family to learn the essentials of chivalry and courtesy. Again, we have no means of knowing if this happened to Henry.

Looking at his childhood from the other angle we may also be wide of the mark if we assume that his entry into holy orders was unwilling, imparting a character into which he grew, if at all, only as the years went by. Recent English history offers many examples of men whose call to the profession of arms and subsequent vocation to the ordained ministry have seemed equally genuine and their success therein equally marked. Some modern thinking may regard these calls as totally incompatible, even in conditions such as those of the two world wars where many achieved distinction before being set free to follow their main vocation; one could certainly argue that Henry Despenser was not necessarily hypocritical in uniting the callings of a soldier and a priest.[27] After all, this is to some extent what the Knights Templar did before they were so brutally suppressed in the early years of the fourteenth century.

The decision that Henry should become a churchman was made very early, for when he was only eleven, on 2 August 1354, he was made Canon of Salisbury by papal provision, with expectation of a prebend, at the petition of his brother Edward.[28] More preferment followed. On 20 January 1361, he was granted a papal dispensation to hold a benefice with cure of souls, and this duly arrived when his brother Edward presented him to the rectory of Bosworth in Leicestershire on 22 December in the same year.[29] Only on 17 December 1362 was he ordained subdeacon in the diocese of Worcester.[30] It would appear that, like his friend Thomas Arundel, he was not ordained deacon or priest until just before his consecration as bishop.

In April 1364, a regular torrent of preferment flowed in. Henry received a canonry of Lincoln, with expectation of a prebend, and also became Rector of Elsworth in Cambridgeshire. Next came an even higher honour, the Arch-deaconry of Llandaff, which the Pope permitted him to hold with one or other of his existing benefices with cure. This connection with Llandaff fitted in very well with the existing family interests in South Wales. Two years later, in 1366, the long-awaited prebend at Salisbury was granted, and was augmented, in the same year, by a canonry and prebend at Llandaff.[31]

As a mere subdeacon Henry could not have fulfilled any of these posts in person. They were merely sources of income to be served by deputy. There was, in fact, a compelling reason why he should not yet be ordained priest. By the decree *Super Pecula* priests were debarred from studying civil law unless given dispensation by the Pope,[32] and Henry had taken up that very subject at Oxford.

When, in January 1361, Henry had received papal dispensation to hold a benefice with cure of souls, he was described as a scholar of civil law. Later in the same year he became B.C.L., and by the time of his consecration he was a licentiate. This was an intermediate grade between bachelor and doctor. His exact scholastic timetable cannot be disentangled; the only clear fact is that no one could be presented for the licence until they had completed six years in the faculty. But we may be sure that, like everything else in Henry's life, his academic career started distinctly early. He was a B.C.L. at 18; and besides the years of study required for that he had to undergo an arts course first, though there is evidence that for intending civil lawyers this requirement could be considerably truncated.[33]

It is therefore clear that Bishop Henry was not the loutish and aristocratic ignoramus later depicted by hostile monks.[34] On the contrary he seems to have been clever and precocious, though precocity was needed if one was to reach the top of a profession or calling in times when the average expectation of life was far lower than it is now. Hobbes' dictum about life being 'nasty, brutish and short' was even more true of the fourteenth century than it was when he wrote in the seventeenth.

At the same time cleverness and precocity can express themselves through irresponsibility and – if the word may be excused – sheer bloody-mindedness. Henry's enthusiasm for legal combat and his own episcopal rights sometimes came very close to this; but we have to remember that the later Middle Ages were excessively litigious times, when those with rights and privileges frequently had to defend them against others, while going on the offensive themselves whenever an opportunity presented itself.

The monks may not have known of Bishop Henry's academic career; but even if they had they would probably have shifted their ground and vented the habitual theologian's scorn for people like ecclesiastical and civil lawyers who studied to gain money and lucrative offices rather than for the pure love of God. But this appears to have been a view largely confined to themselves. For C. J. Godfrey's researches show beyond doubt that civil law was by far the most popular academic study in the fourteenth century.[35] To use his own words: 'It was above all legal qualification which opened the door to ecclesiastical promotion.' Thus among 27 pluralist graduates in the diocese of London in 1366 lawyers easily predominated over theologians, while out of 140 graduates from the other dioceses no less than 80 were lawyers, 45 M.A.s, ten theologians and four medical doctors, while one held dual qualifications in medicine and law. Higher theological studies were in fact confined to Paris, Oxford and Cambridge until a new faculty of theology was authorised at Toulouse by Pope Innocent VI.[36]

Another interesting point brought out by Godfrey is that Archbishop Courtenay was only 'in legibus licentiatus'. It may well be that the licentiate was as far as a potential bishop needed to go, while those looking towards teaching or advocacy would aspire to a doctorate in one or both of the legal faculties.[37]

Other questions are not so easily answered. One would like to know something about Henry's life at Oxford as a student and a young graduate. Not surprisingly nothing survives, though it may be assumed that his rank exempted him from the hardships experienced by those with little money and no connections. Above all we should like to discover whether at this stage he belonged to the newly-founded Queen's College,[38] for at the end of his life he rented rooms there when, in a manner more familiar today, he returned to his studies and his university. Workman speaks of an interest he had acquired in collecting versions of metrical prophecies.[39]

By the late 1360s Henry had acquired a university education and a valuable collection of ecclesiastical benefices and dignities. He may also have acquired, albeit unofficially, a measure of skill at arms. Then, in 1368, his brother Edward announced that he was to visit Italy in the retinue of Lionel, Duke of Clarence, and with his career awaiting its next move Henry may well have found the chance of accompanying him attractive.

The purpose of Lionel of Clarence's visit was to marry Violante, the daughter of Galeazzo Visconti, Lord of Pavia, the ambitious younger brother of Bernabo Visconti, Duke of Milan. The marriage duly took place amid great splendour, feasting and tournaments, but was followed only five months later by Clarence's death – or, as some thought, murder.[40] This meant, in effect, that the Despenser brothers had to go home or find something else to do. The latter in fact presented few difficulties, though it is likely that they had to keep the government at home aware of what they were doing and obtain formal permission.[41]

Free companies of mercenary soldiers had become a feature of life in France during the previous twenty years. They thrived on war, but when there was no war they still had to live. This they did by terrorising towns and villages - even cities as important as Avignon – and collecting plunder and cash payments to induce them to go away. Chivalry meant nothing to them; they were no more than bandits and gangsters. In the course of time some ventured further afield and found congenial employment in Italy. John Capgrave speaks of 'Ser John Hawkwood, a marvelous man of armes, which led in Itale a grete cumpany clepit "The White Felauchip". His dedes wold ask a special tretys.'[42] In Italy Hawk-wood spent the remainder of his life.

Indeed the life of this kind of mercenary had much to commend it. Employment was readily to hand in a country fragmented into many juris-dictions, secular and spiritual, and it had the advantage of being not too dangerous. After all, your adversary of today might be your ally of tomorrow, so when you met him in combat it was best not to be too violent or brutal. The object in battle was to manoeuvre your opponent into an untenable position, at which point he would surrender. So the most unpleasant consequence of defeat would be a spell in prison not unduly protracted.

Being perhaps somewhat disillusioned with the Visconti, Edward and Henry enrolled themselves in the crusade which Pope Urban V had proclaimed against Bernabo in Lombardy.[43] Whether the same not over-active style of warfare prevailed when a crusade was in progress we do not know; but in any case the brothers greatly distinguished themselves, so much so that the Pope was moved to write to John of Gaunt asking him to commend Edward to his father the king, as having won a glorious name in the battles of Lombardy.[44] As for Henry his contribution seems also to have been outstanding, for Capgrave mentions him alongside the renowned Sir John Hawkwood himself.

> 'In this same tyme was Ser Herry Spenser a grete werrioure in Itaile, or the time that he was promoted.'[45]

Corroborative evidence comes from Froissart, who was well acquainted with the family.[46]

Of particular interest is the statement that Henry, like his four brothers, had already been advanced to the dignity of knighthood. His subdeacon's orders and archdeaconry of Llandaff were not, in themselves, a total bar to this, and the knighthood is unlikely to have come from Edward III himself. The theory that Capgrave is confusing Henry with Edward seems disproved by his specific words 'or the time that he was promoted'.[47]

For in 1370 the promotion came. Perhaps – who knows? – Henry's military success under the guidance of such eminent tutors had made him doubtful as to which path he should follow. Should it still be a call to the ordained ministry of the Church or a call to the profession of arms? At least one other well-born youth had experienced such a crisis of conscience. William Beauchamp, a son of the Earl of Warwick, had given up a promising career in the Church in order to follow a military life. Did other young men from aristocratic families delay ordination and so keep their options open?

But Beauchamp did not have the Pope to deal with. Urban V clearly wanted Henry, this promising young man, to give leadership as a soldier of Christ; and he therefore provided him to the bishopric of Norwich, vacant by the death of Thomas Percy, when he was still over three years below the canonical age for consecration, which was thirty. It is easy to point the finger of criticism at Urban. But he would have known his man; and as for his spirituality he was the only pope to be granted - posthumously, of course - the rank of Blessed during the whole of the fourteenth century.

Notes

1. Froissart: *Chronicles,* ed. Kervyn de Lettenhove, Brussels, 1870-1877, vol. 1, p. 143.

2. *Complete Peerage,* London, 1916, vol. 4, pp. 259-260, 287. The more famous family of Stuart began in much the same way.

3. For example in 1401, when the bishop is referred to as 'Reverent pere en Dieu et notre trescher cousin'. *Proceedings and Ordinances of the Privy Council of England,* 10 Richard II to 11 Henry IV (1386-1410), ed. Sir Harris Nicholas, 1834, p. 167.

4. Ezekiel 18, especially verses 14 to 18.

5. *Complete Peerage,* vol. 4, pp. 271-274 and references there cited.

6. *Dictionary of National Biography,* vol. XIV, pp. 410-412. Entry for Henry Despenser.

7. Froissart says expressly that there were only four sons, but this is inaccurate. D.N.B. entry ut supra (note 2).

8. *Calendar of Papal Registers,* Papal Letters, vol. 3, 1362-1396, p. 83.

9. Froissart: *Chronicles,* vol. I, p. 147, cf. vol. 8, p. 312. For Froissart's tribute to Edward Le Despenser I have used the translation by Geoffrey Brereton in Froissart, *Chronicles,* Harmondsworth, 1968, p. 192.

10. For example Sir Thomas Despenser held two-thirds of the manor of Essendine in Rutland for life by demise of Edward, together with property at Bourne in Lincolnshire and Buckland with 'Syncleburgh' (Syndercombe?) in Buckinghamshire. *Inquisitions Post Mortem,* vol. XV, 1-7 Richard II, 1970, pp. 138ff.

11. As explained to me by The Very Reverend Michael Moxon, Dean of Truro, formerly Vicar of Tewkesbury, who was able to see the effigy at close quarters during the restoration.

12. This is the Northampton Inquisition Post Mortem. The Solihull inquisition says 22. For Hugh see I.P.M. vol. XIV (1374-1377) pp. 51-52. For his wife Alice see I.P.M. vol. XV (1-7 Richard II) p. 92.

13. He had earlier visited Prussia, when he had with him three esquires and four yeomen. He carried two letters from his brother Edward, perhaps of introduction, and was to receive a sum of money 'in the parts beyond seas' and £20 for his expenses. C.P.R. 1367-1370, p. 58. Perhaps, like many others, he was seeking military experience with the Teutonic Knights.

14. Froissart: *Chronicles,* vol. 8, p. 295.

15. For example: C.P.R., 1361-1364, pp. 409, 423: 1364-1367, p. 57: 1367-1370, p. 219 (where Thomas is 'the king's kinsman'): 1377-1381, p. 452.

16. *I.P.M.,* vol. XV, pp. 138-139.

17. *C.P.R.,* 1367-1370, p. 132.

18. *C.P.R.,* 1381-1385, p. 363.

19. *I.P.M.,* vol. XV, pp. 235-236.

20. Ibid, p. 236.

21. E. F. Jacob, *The Fifteenth Century,* Oxford, 1961, p. 25.

22. *Calendar of Inquisitions Miscellaneous,* 1399-1422, pp. 253-254.

23. *Complete Peerage,* vol. IV, pp. 280-281, quoting Parliamentary Rolls, vol. 3, p. 459 and vol. 5, p. 484.

24. *I.P.M.,* vol. XIV, pp. 214-227 and vol.XVI (7-15 Richard II), p. 206. For his Irish possessions see C.P.R., 1370-1374, p. 285. Because of his absence in Lombardy at the king's order he is excused the forfeiture of his Irish lands, though he has not gone to the defence of the king's interests there, or sent others in his place, as required of all English landholders.

25. *Abstracts of Inquisitions Post Mortem for Gloucestershire 1359-1413,* ed. Ethel Stokes, British Record Society, 1914, pp. 95-96.

26. *The Canterbury Tales,* from the poetical works of Geoffrey Chaucer, World's Classics, Oxford, 1930, pp. 2-3.

27. For a further discussion of this subject see below, pp. 43-44.

28. *A Biographical Register of the University of Oxford to 1500,* ed. A. B. Emden, Oxford, 1957, vol. 3, Appendix 2, pp. 2169-2170, with references there cited.

29. For Edward's right to present see *I.P.M.,* vol. XIV (1374-1377), pp. 214-227 under Additional Inquisitions: Leicester (Boseworth). He held the advowson in right of Elizabeth his wife.

30. Emden, op cit.

31. Ibid. Appendix 2 details 'those not positively known to have studied at Oxford or Cambridge, but of whom it is fair to assume that a substantial proportion pursued at least part of their academical studies at Oxford.' Emden is, however, unaware of Bishop Henry's connection with Queen's College, Oxford at the end of his life, which may indicate that he was an Oxford man.

32. *History of the University of Oxford,* ed. J. I. Catto, Oxford, 1984, p. 540.

33. Catto, op cit. p. 370. This may be why he is not described as Master.

34. For example in Walsingham, *Chronicon Angliæ,* ed. E. Maunde Thompson, Rolls Series, 1874, p. 258.

35. C. J. Godfrey, 'Pluralists in the Province of Canterbury in 1366', in *Journal of Ecclesiastical History,* 1960, pp. 23-40.

36. Godfrey, op cit., pp. 33-34.

37. Ibid, p. 31.

38. J. R. Magrath, *The Queen's College,* 1921, vol. I, p. 131, note 5.

39. H. B. Workman, *John Wyclif,* Oxford, 1926, p. 69.

40. *Chronicon Henrici Knighton, Monachi Leycestrensis,* ed. J. R. Lumby, Rolls Series, 1895, vol. 2, p. 123. 'Et ibi aliquamdiu moram trahens intoxicatus veneno interiit'. He was buried at Pavia near the tomb of St Augustine. (John Capgrave, *Chronicle of England,* p. 225) See also D. Pearsall, *The Life of Geoffrey Chaucer,* Oxford, 1992, p. 53.

41. See note 24 above.

42. Capgrave, op. cit., p. 226.

43. N. Housley, 'The Bishop of Norwich's Crusade', May, 1383, in *History Today,* May 1983, p. 16.

44. *Calendar of Papal Letters,* IV, p. 28.

45. Capgrave, op cit., p. 226.

46. Froissart: *Chronicles,* vols. VII, p. 251 and X, p. 210.

47. Emden, op cit., vol. I, pp. 138-139, quoted in W. M. Ormrod, *The Reign of Edward III,* 1990, p. 132.

2. The Bishop in his Diocese

There is no evidence that the new Bishop of Norwich had ever visited East Anglia. As we have seen the family power-base was in the West Country and South Wales; and even his brothers' possessions in the Midlands were the best part of a hundred miles from his new diocese. Even so, he appears to have been in no hurry to take up his new and important task. Some bishops of the time rarely went near their dioceses, often because they were busy at a high level in the service of the crown and the church. It soon became clear that Bishop Henry was not to be one of these. Nevertheless the first episcopal act recorded in his register was the institution of John Auty to the rectory of Wenham Parva on 2 August 1372, two years after his appointment.[1]

Where had he been in the meantime? The veil lifts only twice. On 12 December 1370 a commission sent by him to Norwich reveals that he was *'apud castrum de Henle'*.[2] This was the castle of Henley in Arden in Warwickshire, otherwise known as Beaudesert, a Despenser possession, where King Edward III is known to have stayed a few months later.[3] At about the same time he and his brother Edward are known to have taken part in the baptism of one Edward Carent at Hanley near Upton-on-Severn.[4]

Meanwhile, awaiting him at Norwich was the magnificent cathedral church of the Holy Trinity in which his episcopal throne was set. In 1096, soon after his see was transferred from Thetford to Norwich, Bishop Herbert de Losinga, one of the great Norman building bishops, had begun the construction of a vast church and a range of buildings to accommodate a priory of sixty Benedictine monks. Not content with that, he established subordinate houses at Lynn and Great Yarmouth, both with splendid churches of their own.

This cathedral had changed comparatively little by the time Henry Despenser became bishop. The saintly Bishop Suffield had erected a Lady Chapel at the east end midway through the thirteenth century, and Thomas Percy, Henry's immediate predecessor, had remodelled the eastern arm in a style reflecting the transition from the Decorated to the Perpendicular style of Gothic architecture. The task of rebuilding the monastic cloisters was proceeding slowly, only to be finished in the next century. But in all essentials the great church remained thoroughly Norman.

For Bishop Henry, however, concern for buildings needed to be matched by an equal, if not greater, concern for the welfare of those who lived in them. By an unusual arrangement, peculiar to England and parts of France, some cathedrals were staffed by a prior and monks instead of the more usual dean and canons. As already mentioned, Bishop Herbert de Losinga had introduced this arrangement at Norwich. Such a scheme could work very well if the bishop, like Herbert, happened to be a monk himself and in sympathy with the monastic ideal. He could then, to some extent, act as abbot of the community. But if, like Bishop Henry, he was not a monk there was room for all kinds of misunderstanding and friction. In the event, Henry was involved in a legal battle with his cathedral priory for most of his episcopate, a battle that was the despair of those who sought to arbitrate and which was left unresolved at his death.

The monks of a cathedral priory possessed considerable powers. They had the right of electing a new bishop when a vacancy occurred, though in practice this right was frequently set aside by the pope or the king, or a combination of both. They did in fact elect their long-serving prior, Alexander Totington, when Henry died in 1406. But in so doing they infuriated Henry IV, who put the unfortunate prior in prison until the Archbishop of Canterbury, Thomas Arundel, finally persuaded the king to accept him.

Like the dean of an ordinary 'secular' cathedral the prior had the right to perform the enthronement of a new bishop. So Prior Nicholas de Hoo, whom he found in office, would have enthroned Bishop Henry Despenser; but we do not know if he came to Norwich for his enthronement immediately after his appointment in 1370, or whether he deferred it until he began to be active in the diocese two years later. Whenever it was, it would have been a colourful and impressive ceremony which Henry, himself a colourful personality, would probably have enjoyed.

Enthronement, however, was only the last of the acts that needed to be performed before Henry could enjoy his bishopric of Norwich with all its rights and privileges. His consecration, carried out at Rome on 20 April 1370, was necessarily preceded by his ordination to the diaconate and the priesthood.[5] Next he received the spiritualities of his see, the right to exercise episcopal authority, from William Whittlesey, Archbishop of Canterbury, on 12 July.[6] Finally Edward III handed over the temporalities, the actual possessions that went with the bishopric, on 14 August in the same year.[7] But this was conditional upon Henry solemnly renouncing all words in the papal bull of provision that might be prejudicial to the king and his authority.

What exactly did he receive? In the fourteenth century the Bishop of Norwich was responsible for the spiritual welfare of the two counties of Norfolk and Suffolk, comprising the archdeaconries of Norwich, Norfolk, Suffolk and Sudbury, and over thirteen hundred parishes.[8] Some of these parishes have ceased to exist through pestilence, movement of population or enclosure, while others, notably Dunwich, have fallen victim to the incursions of the sea. But the majority are still to be found, and in spite of differences in spelling can be identified in the bishop's immense register, extending through the entire thirty-six years of his episcopate.[9] In addition there were more than eighty monasteries and nunneries within the diocesan boundaries.[10] A few of these were exempt from his jurisdiction, for example the great abbey of St Edmundsbury, the priory of Wymondham, dependent upon St Albans Abbey, and the priories of Thetford and Castle Acre, houses of the international Order ruled from Cluny in France. But the majority, many of them small Augustinian houses of regular canons, were a responsibility that could be both onerous and unwelcome.

For the youngest son of a middle-ranking baronial family the temporal possessions Henry Despenser received with his bishopric – land, property, rents, privileges and the like – were lucrative and very extensive. How much were they worth? When he lost them in 1383, after the failure of the Flanders Crusade, they were granted to Sir Richard Waldegrave, Sir Edmund de Thorpe, William Wynter and Robert Wayte for a rent of 500 marks a year, though they were not to receive the profits from knights' fees or the advowsons of churches. In 1385 Michael de la Pole, Earl of Suffolk, estimated the temporalities to be worth a clear £1,000 a year. To sustain his earldom the king had granted him 1,000 marks per annum, only two-thirds of what the bishop was accustomed to receive – if his estimate was accurate. Much later, in 1535, the *Valor Ecclesiasticus* commissioned by Henry VIII gave the income of the bishopric as £979. But comparison with statistics given by the late Dr Virgoe regarding the assets of the cathedral priory at various times in the later Middle Ages suggests that during Henry Despenser's episcopate the bishopric might have been worth con-siderably more than that.[11]

Henry also found himself the owner of several residences, though we are told that during the interregnum local people had made off with many of the doors and windows of his manor houses.[12] His main episcopal palace was next to the cathedral; but not far away, on the road to Great Yarmouth and close to the river Yare, was the manor of Thorpe Episcopi. Further out in the same direction was Blofield which, in common with Eccles near Thetford, possessed a warren, a valuable asset for the maintenance of a large household.[13] Thornage near Holt and Hevingham to the south of Aylsham were also episcopal possessions, both equipped with game-parks for the aristocratic pursuit of hunting. Further to the west was North Elmham, where the cathedral of the diocese had once stood, situated between Dereham and Fakenham. Finally there was Gaywood on the outskirts of King's Lynn – or as it was in those days, Bishop's Lynn.

Most strategically-placed of all were the two manors of South Elmham and Hoxne in the Waveney valley. From these, aided by monastic hospitality at Ipswich and elsewhere, Bishop Henry could cover the Suffolk part of his diocese and yet be reasonably close to headquarters at Norwich. At South Elmham the moated manor house still exists. Both the Elmhams and Hoxne had been associated with the East Anglian diocese in Anglo-Saxon times, and at North Elmham[14] the remains of the ancient cathedral were incorporated into the episcopal dwelling.[15] South Elmham and Hoxne were also useful staging posts when the Bishop had to travel to London.[16] There, like most of his colleagues, he maintained a considerable establishment. His hospice, as it was called, was in the village of Charing between the City and Westminster.[17] The list of his possessions is completed by the manors of Maudittes at Terling and Le Bysshopeshall at Lambourn, both in Essex. To judge from his register Bishop Henry used them very little. He visited Terling for six weeks in 1377, and Lambourn not at all.

During his long episcopate (1370-1406) different manor houses were in favour at different times. Hoxne appears frequently in the register during 1373 and 1388, while from 1380 onwards South Elmham is often preferred. Blofield had a period of popularity in the late 1370s, but in the final years of his life Bishop Henry resided almost exclusively at North Elmham. He was also in London, the seat of the royal administration, as well as in Norwich. After the failure of the Flanders Crusade in 1383[18] he stayed in Norwich almost continually until late 1387. This may in part have been due to the loss of his temporalities and the consequent denial of access to his manors but, as will be suggested later, there may have been other reasons also. The years 1390 to 1393 saw another prolonged period of residence at Norwich. From 1377 to 1382 Bishop Henry is occasionally found at Thorpe Episcopi, and it is possible that in later years his registrar did not differentiate between his house there and his palace in the city nearby. Thornage, Hevingham, Eccles and Gaywood do not seem to have aroused much enthusiasm, though in the case of the latter the Bishop's strained relations with the people of Lynn may have been a contributing factor.

When Henry lost his temporalities in 1383 the government saw to it that those holding office in the manors in his name should not be affected. William Cursoun of Billingford, the royal escheator for Norfolk,[19] was in overall charge, but Geoffrey Atkyn, the Bishop's esquire, was confirmed in office as master and surveyor of all the parks, woods, warrens, chases and fisheries normally in episcopal possession. Any esquire of Bishop Henry could never rule out the possibility of fighting but it is, perhaps, more likely that Geoffrey was a mature man from the increasing class of gentlefolk who had no desire to proceed to knighthood. Together with Geoffrey, named individuals are confirmed as custodians of the parks and warrens of Blofield, Thornage, South Elmham, Eccles, Hevingham and Hoxne.[20]

Alongside the master and surveyor there was a steward. On March 1, 1384, Robert Cayly was confirmed in the office of steward of all the Bishop's manors in Norfolk and Suffolk at a yearly salary of twenty marks. The original grant, for life, had been made by Bishop Henry in April, 1380.[21] Here again the status quo is being maintained while the temporalities are in the king's hands, and for good measure Cayly is also appointed, during the royal pleasure, as steward of the town of Lynn Episcopi. This was another regular post in the episcopal administration.[22]

There is also evidence for the existence of a receiver, who handled revenues sent in from the various manors. But the person concerned, Robert Barbour of Huntingdon, appears to have been thoroughly unsatisfactory. In October 1381, he is being pressed to render accounts for the time he held office, while five years later he is under increasing pressure, for he is now in debt to others beside the bishop.[23]

Yet another servant, presumably clerical, was the Official of the Manorial Jurisdiction'. It was his duty to induct, in place of the local archdeacon, clergy appointed by the bishop to benefices on his personal lands and in his direct gift or collation. These included Blofield and Beighton not far from Norwich, Blickling to the north of the county and several churches in the area of South Elmham, including the nunnery of Flixton. Another Official, based at Lynn, undertook similar duties there.[24] It is interesting that the prior and convent of the cathedral had a similar functionary, the Dean of the Manors, who likewise inducted clerks into benefices on their lands and in their gift.[25] On one occasion, during his dispute with the monks, the Bishop himself gave offence by having John Waryn inducted into the vicarage of Trowse, a right which properly belonged to the Dean of the Manors.

Under these more senior servants humbler members of the bishop's workforce laboured in obscurity with the single exception of John Drolle, a bondman of South Elmham, who was granted his freedom, together with all his issue, by Bishop Henry on 5 December, 1382. This transaction, which needed the approval of the prior and convent of the cathedral priory, was confirmed fourteen years later, presumably at Drolle's request. Other would-be freemen had been less fortunate. In 1360, before Bishop Henry's time, two other South Elmham serfs had claimed their freedom. But John Clench and John Soule ended up in the stocks and had to pay a fine of three shillings and four pence each.[26]

These matter-of-fact records tell us nothing of the bishop's relationship with those who worked on his manors and, in many cases, did not see him very often. In contrast to what might be assumed from some of his other actions, his reputation as a caring bishop is also emphasised. John Capgrave goes so far as to say that he retained the heartfelt respect of all who served him – 'omnium subditorium corda retinuit'.[27] This is certainly borne out by the information we

17

have about the clerks who worked with him in the administration of the diocese. Two of them stayed with him for the entire thirty-six years of his episcopate.

Strictly speaking Master John Darlington was not appointed at the beginning of Bishop Henry's tenure in 1370. He was confirmed as Vicar-General in September 1371, almost a year before the bishop arrived in his diocese.[28] This commission associates him with Prior Nicholas of the cathedral monastery, who had previously acted with Master Roger Yonge de Sutton, Keeper of the Spiritualities during the recent vacancy in the see.[29]

John Darlington was a younger contemporary of Bishop Henry at Oxford, and they may well have become friends there, although Darlington preferred canon law to the civil law studied by the bishop. He was bachelor of canon law at the end of 1363, had his licentiate by 1371 and his doctorate by early 1382.[30]

During the later Middle Ages a diocesan bishop usually employed two senior deputies, though sometimes the offices were combined. One was the Vicar-General, who could deal with all the bishop's pastoral and administrative work apart from matters specifically requiring episcopal orders. The bishop usually reserved to himself collations to benefices in his personal gift. The other deputy was the Official Principal, who exercised his legal jurisdiction and presided over the consistory court of the diocese. In Despenser's register John Darlington is sometimes called Vicar-General, sometimes Official Principal. The explanation is that his basic responsibility was to be Official Principal, an office which needed to be held continuously, but that from time to time he was also made Vicar-General while the bishop was absent from his diocese, or even occasionally when he was not. In line with the usual practice at that time Darlington's commissions as Vicar-General, of which there are many, give no signs of permanent tenure. Sometimes others are appointed alongside him or in his place. But as the years go by it becomes increasingly obvious that John Darlington was Bishop Henry's right-hand man, who occupied a place in his counsels and his affections above all others.[31]

A testimony to Darlington's worth comes in a letter from Thomas, Lord Morley to Thomas Arundel, Archbishop of Canterbury, assigned by Miss Legge to 1405-1406.[32] Morley asks the archbishop to mediate between his kinsman the bishop and Master John Rickinghall, dean of the collegiate church of St Mary-in-the-Fields at Norwich.[33] Both parties had already accepted John Darlington's arbitration, but Master Henry Well, a former dean of the college, had persuaded the bishop to go back on his agreement. Morley, who has also been trying to mediate at the archbishop's request, is very concerned about the future of St Mary-in-the-Fields, which is far from rich, but states specifically that Rickinghall is quite ready to accept Darlington's arbitration though he is fully

18

aware that Darlington is close to the bishop.[34] One gains a clear impression of a man both upright and vastly experienced, respected by all.

He was well rewarded for his service, even at an early stage in their relationship. On 1st October 1372, he was appointed Master of St Giles' Hospital (the Great Hospital) in Norwich, a post that was becoming – not in line with the founder's wishes – the preserve of senior diocesan administrators. In 1375 he received the benefices of Great Massingham and Hingham, in 1376 he was holding a prebend in St Mary-in-the-Fields, and finally, in 1387, he became Archdeacon of Norwich.[35] The bishop had the right of collation to all the dignities and prebends at St Mary-in-the-Fields, which was a useful way of rewarding his servants. For, as his cathedral was monastic, he had no patronage there.

Although John Darlington was Master of St Giles' Hospital for little more than three years, his successor being appointed on 5 January, 1376,[36] the bell tower that still exists there is called Darlington's Tower. Built in 1396-1397, twenty years after his mastership, his gift of £23 made its completion possible: and although it is modest compared with the soaring tower and spire of the cathedral nearby, in its unobtrusive solidity it is a fitting memorial to the man from whom it takes its name. Darlington in fact outlived his master, for he and

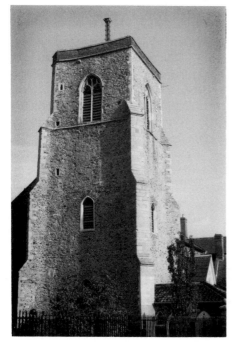

Darlington's Tower,
St Giles' Hospital, Norwich

William Milton acted as keepers of the spiritualities of the diocese during the ensuing vacancy. Later still, in 1410, he gave St Giles' Hospital a most generous legacy consisting of the manor of Cringleford and the advowson of the church of Wickmere near Aylsham. The masses and prayers he asked for his soul should have been gladly offered.[37] Indeed the thriving establishment now known as the Great Hospital also has every reason to be grateful to such a benefactor.

It would appear that during the earlier part of his career John Darlington had served as a king's clerk,[38] but the extent of his work for the bishop and diocese as the perfect second-in-command would almost certainly have precluded such activity later on. In this he differs from other distinguished people we find serving Bishop Henry. Some of these made significant contributions; but they also had interests and responsibilities elsewhere.

Several of these prominent clerks bear names that might be of East Anglian origin. Thomas Hethersett came from the village of that name just to the south-west of Norwich; and although there are Carletons all over England William of that name might have belonged to East Carleton in the same area as Hethersett. John Freton may have hailed from Fritton near St Olave's in Suffolk or another Fritton in the countryside between Norwich and Diss. In both cases Freton is identical with a medieval spelling given by Ekwall.[39] Most distinctive and obvious of all is the name of Master John Rickinghall, who has already been mentioned. The twin villages of Rickinghall Superior and Inferior lie on the main A43 road between Diss and Bury St. Edmunds, and his origins can certainly be traced to there. For that matter his adversary Henry Well may have been a native of Wells-next-the-Sea on Norfolk's north coast; but the less distinctive the name the less possible it is to establish its provenance with any certainty.

Bishop Henry gave employment and benefices to many clerks. But it might be instructive to concentrate on the five just mentioned. Of these Thomas Hethersett had a distinguished career at Cambridge. Bachelor of Civil Law by 1370, he had his doctorate by 1385, in which year he became Warden of King's Hall. The following year he was Chancellor of the University.[40] Soon afterwards he begins to appear in Despenser's register, usually entrusted with special commissions,[41] and it is not long before he is appointed Archdeacon of Sudbury by Richard II. This position he held, with one short break, until his death in 1406. But as with all archdeacons of this period one asks to what extent, if at all, he gave personal attention to his official duties.

Rather less is known about Master William Carleton. Doubly qualified, with doctorates in both civil and canon law, he was employed by Bishop Henry as Vicar-General on numerous occasions and was also entrusted with special commissions. As a reward for his labours he received the rectories of Blickling and Blofield, both in the bishop's personal gift.[42] Blofield, in fact, was given to a whole succession of his senior clerks, all of whom were duly inducted by the official of the manorial jurisdiction. After Despenser's death Carleton was one of the lawyers involved in the composition effected by Archbishop Arundel between Bishop Totington and the prior and convent of the cathedral in 1411.[43]

John Freton's attainments were more modest, though he may have been related to Roger Freton, D.C.L., who held three canonries, the archdeaconry of Essex and the deanery of Chichester before his death in 1382.[44] By contrast John does not seem to have attended a university. He was, however, a king's clerk who received a royal presentation to the archdeaconry of Norfolk in March, 1374.[45] But there was a dispute over this presentation, the bishop having also put up a candidate, and Freton was not instituted until almost a year later.[46] In April 1377, he is referred to in legal proceedings as 'clerk of Corston', which may be Corton, a village on the coast between Great Yarmouth and Lowestoft, the rectory of which was annexed to that archdeaconry.[47] In September 1389, he became Precentor of St Mary-in-the-Fields[48] and finally, in November 1400, we find him instituted to the vicarage of Thornham, near Hunstanton, taking the usual oath of personal residence required in such cases.[49] It seems that in contrast to his highly successful relative John Freton's career never really 'took off', at least in worldly terms, though his acceptance of a humble cure of souls at Thornham may indicate that he had a deeper sense of priesthood. Not all the senior clergy of the time were inveterate place-seekers and accumulators of ecclesiastical dignities.[50]

Very different was the life of John Rickinghall. Already an acolyte by 1376 he may have been born about 1360. From 1381 he began to acquire an impressive collection of preferments of which the earlier ones may have been intended to support his university career at Cambridge. By 1405 he was master of arts and doctor of theology; ten years later he was Chancellor of the University, and the year after that Master of Gonville Hall. In the diocese of Norwich he acted as Henry Despenser's commissary in July 1400,[51] having become Dean of St Mary-in-the-Fields in 1395. In 1400 he relinquished this in favour of Henry Well, but in 1405 he was re-appointed and served for another twenty-one years, thus confirming the care and interest we have already noticed in his dealings with that college. Elsewhere he was Archdeacon of Northumberland and Chancellor of York Minster, but had to give up his whole portfolio of preferments on becoming Bishop of Chichester early in 1426. In the same year he acted as confessor to John, Duke of Bedford, and between 1427 and 1428 was Henry VI's proctor at the papal court in Rome. By now, however, he

21

had either attained or was approaching the age of seventy, rather too late to be made a bishop, and in 1429 he died and was buried in the north choir aisle of his cathedral church.[52]

As suggested above, there seems to have been no love lost between John Rickinghall and Henry Well, at least in the opinion of Lord Morley. Another Cambridge man, Well had his bachelor's degree in canon law by 1389 and his licentiate in 1414. During the final decade of the fourteenth century he held benefices in Ely and Norwich dioceses including Beighton, in Bishop Despenser's own gift, Barton Turf and Grimston. Next came the deanery of St Mary-in-the-Fields, followed in 1404 by the rectory of Great Cressingham, a remote place but well endowed and given in succession to various senior clergy in the bishop's service. In the register entry referring to this he is described as 'Master Henry Walton, otherwise called Well'.[53] Finally, in the year following Despenser's death, he became Archdeacon of Lincoln and remained in that office until he died in about 1431, when his body was brought back to Norfolk to be buried in West Dereham Abbey. From 1413 until at least 1416 he had been Master of Trinity Hall at Cambridge, and a few years later contributed the generous sum of £40 towards the finishing of the cloisters at Norwich Cathedral.[54]

With four archdeaconries in his diocese, and an episcopate of thirty-six years, Bishop Henry had dealings with many archdeacons. A few may have carried out their duties in person but most, one suspects, saw their office as a source of revenue not requiring residence, just as the Bishop himself had seen the archdeaconry of Llandaff. A good example of this class was Richard Mitford, presented by the king to the archdeaconry of Norfolk on August 18, 1385.[55] Mitford became Bishop of Chichester in 1388 and was translated to Salisbury in 1395. Occasionally a faithful servant was rewarded. Robert Foulmere had been the bishop's war treasurer during the Flemish Crusade. Like his master he ran into considerable trouble afterwards, being accused of misappropriating 5,000 francs received from the French.[56] But in July 1387, the bishop appointed him to the archdeaconry of Suffolk, which he held for three years before exchanging it with John Thorp for a canonry in the king's free chapel of St Stephen at Westminster, and the rectory of Fawley in Hampshire.[57] Clearly his career had suffered no more than a momentary hiccup. Indeed he was so friendly with his bishop that on more than one occasion the latter used his house at Westminster when his own was not available. Later he became one of the many administrators to hold the rectory of Blofield, and in the same year, 1401, he was given papal permission for life to enjoy the fruits of his benefice while studying at a university. He had gained a master's degree eleven years before but his renewed studies, if they happened at all, lasted for only a few months as he was dead by September, 1401.[58]

Perhaps the most colourful of Despenser's archdeacons was Dr Eudo La Zouche, an elderly civil lawyer who was given Sudbury shortly before the bishop's death. This unusual and aristocratic name completely defeated the episcopal registrar, who first rendered it as 'La Senche' and needed another try before he got it right.[59]

Undoubtedly the most devious of the Norwich archdeacons of this time was Master William Northwold, who is said to have been Archdeacon of Sudbury for seven years. But it is far from certain that he was ever an archdeacon, or even a master in any university faculty. A vociferous Lollard partisan, his unusual career is discussed below when the Bishop Henry's dealings with heresy are considered.[60]

But what did archdeacons do? They were responsible for the part of the diocese from which they took their title, and an important part of their duties was the enforcement of spiritual discipline in matters of faith and morals. In medieval times they had a very wide authority in such matters, which they exercised through an archidiaconal court subordinate to that of the bishop. Lay officials called summoners assisted them, men who were usually highly unpopular through their intrusion into people's private lives and the suspicion that both they and the archdeacon were too interested in the financial opportunities their work offered. In the *Canterbury Tales* Chaucer's Sompnour puts the matter concisely. 'Purs is the archedeknes hell quod he'.

Other duties that fell to the archdeacon – and in the Church of England still do – were the oversight of churches, parsonage houses and other benefice property to ensure that they were in good repair, and the induction of clergy into the real and corporal possession of the benefices into which they had been instituted. They were also supposed to hold a visitation of their archdeaconry each year, unless the bishop was having one of his own.

With so many non-resident archdeacons it was imperative that there should be an effective deputy to do the work if necessary. In August 1406, just before Bishop Despenser's death, Master Maurice Campeden, bachelor of laws, was Official to the Archdeacon of Norfolk. At that time Campeden was Rector of Foulsham, and four years previously had been instituted to the vicarage of Northales.[61] Earlier he had held the rectory of Belton 'near the sea', and was commissioned to induct Ralph Selby, newly appointed to the archdeaconry of Norfolk, to the annexed living of Corton not far away. This he probably never did, as shortly afterwards he was required to induct Selby's successor and supplanter John Middleton.[62] Other legal officials mentioned in the register may have been Archdeacon's Officials as well, though not referred to as such. Their importance is shown by the sending of mandates for the induction of the newly-beneficed to the appropriate archdeacon 'or his official'.

Indeed, the Archdeacon's Official was a vital cog in the diocesan machine as Norwich, uniquely, does not seem to have had rural deans of the usual kind. He would therefore have dealt directly with a large number of parishes. Deans it did have, but they did not occupy the usual place in the chain of command between the archdeacon and the ordinary parish priest. The office of rural dean, with its task of supervising a number of parishes, has always called for a mature and experienced priest, preferably beneficed, with a close knowledge of the area under his control and the clergy serving there. But in Bishop Henry's day, and indeed for some time before that, the deans were not incumbents and the deaneries were small freehold benefices without cure of souls, given by him to anyone he favoured or who needed funds. Recipients might include diocesan administrators, king's clerks or young students at the university. This he is said to have done out of mere goodwill *(intuiti caritatis)*. Because of the financial aspect the king did not forget them when, after the Flanders Crusade, he held the bishop's temporalities. The register only mentions these deans when they are appointed, there is no suggestion that they carried out any supervision, and we do not even know if there was a house for the dean to live in. The reason for the anomalous position of deans in the diocese of Norwich has never been satisfactorily explained. Perhaps the archdeacons and their officials extended their responsibilities as time went on, and those of the rural deans suffered in consequence.[63]

Well over forty of these deaneries are mentioned in the register. Some appear frequently like Sudbury, Brooke, Ingworth, Depwade, Breckles and Stow; others only once like Fordham, Repps, Dunwich, Flegg and Ipswich. A few bear archaic Saxon names like Thedwardestre and Waxtonesham, reminding us that rural deaneries were often co-terminous with ancient civil areas like hundreds and wapentakes.

Well-qualified clergy were needed for a variety of important functions in the diocese. Regular episcopal visitations were meant to take place but could be performed by deputy. In 1394, for example, Master Thomas Bukton is described as 'our commissary in our ordinary visitation of the archdeaconries of Norwich and Norfolk'.[64] He appears on a panel of legal experts concerned with the right of presentation to the benefice of Walsoken,[65] and he also subscribes to the adjudication by Archbishop Arundel in 1411. Another clerk with a similar name was William Baketon (perhaps from Bacton on the Norfolk coast), who was proctor to the Bishop of Norwich at the Roman court in 1391.[66]

A rather amusing episode shows how Bishop Henry could turn the requirement to hold visitations to his own benefit. After the succession, or usurpation, of Henry IV in 1399 he felt a distinct chilling in the royal attitude. This was hardly surprising as he was known to be a friend and partisan of the former king, and had briefly taken up arms on his behalf. On 1 June 1401, a summons was sent to him from the King requiring his attendance at a Council to be held on the 25th of the same month to consider a dispute between him and the townsfolk of Lynn. Should he be unable to come he was to send representatives to hear what the Council would decide. Bishop Henry replies that attendance is impossible as he is engaged in his visitation of the diocese. This only happens every seven years, and if broken off will result in damage to his episcopal authority. Worse still he is afflicted by gallstones *('cestes diseases novelles de gales')* which have compelled him to return to his manor at North Elmham leaving two of his clerks to proceed with the visitation. He therefore sends, as requested, Master William Sanday, Master James Cole, Sir Robert Foulmere and Master Henry Welles, or two or three of them, to hear the king's will on his behalf. The last two of these we have heard of already. One cannot help wondering whether the gallstones were of the diplomatic variety, for Bishop Henry strongly disapproved of the new king, and did everything he could to avoid meeting him.[67]

The visitations, at least, were genuine for we know they were held in 1394 and 1401. This suggests that in view of the prescribed seven-year interval visitations had also taken place in 1387, 1380 and 1373, which would have been a suitable year for Henry to hold his primary visitation after arrival in his diocese.

As the years go by, new names appear in the episcopal register to denote changes in senior staff. In February 1394, Master Nicholas Stoket, Rector of St Magnus in London, was instituted to the parish of Catton, just north of Norwich, as a special commissioner of Bishop Henry. Almost four years later he is described as 'our Official Principal', which suggests that John Darlington had at last laid down that heavy responsibility.[68]

Then in 1399 the Bishop at last decided to seek help in discharging those duties that required episcopal orders. As we do not have the ordination lists for this period we cannot tell to what extent he had used other bishops on an ad hoc basis both to ordain and to carry out tasks like consecrating churchyards, enclosing anchorites and blessing holy objects of various kinds. But now, after twenty-seven years in the diocese, he enlisted the services of John Leicester, a Carmelite friar who was Archbishop of Smyrna, a titular see in heathen parts *(in partibus infidelium)*, for all that it had once been the second of the Seven Churches written to by St John the Divine.[69] Many suffragan bishops gave help of this kind. Some were accredited to Irish sees too dangerous to visit: others, like Leicester, to areas now dominated by the Turk (Smyrna is now Izmir in

Turkey), and others again to places so outlandish that it is impossible to tell where they were.

On 2 July, 1399, just before the crisis that ended with the deposition of Richard II, the Archbishop of Smyrna was commissioned as a Vicar-General with John Darlington and William Carleton,[70] and in the following year he was given the rectory of Threxton for his support, holding it until 1404.[71] After his appointment John of Smyrna was for a time very active in the diocese, but then he disappears and Bishop Henry takes over again. Of course this does not mean to say that his suffragan was completely set aside. He may have busied himself with other functions that would find no place in the register, which deals mainly with appointments to benefices and religious houses.

We have already seen that at times Henry Despenser remained in his diocese for months and years on end. During other periods the impression given by his register is one of ceaseless, almost frenetic, activity. If its chronology is to be trusted, which is sometimes doubtful, he thought nothing of riding over long distances, and those who formed his inner circle of servants had to be able to do the same. He was certainly not a man who habitually delegated his functions. He delegated when he had to, but the impression given by his register is that he preferred to attend to his responsibilities personally. He never gave anybody, not even John Darlington, a commission to be his permanent vicar-general.

One of the little group that moved around with him was his clerk, who was probably also his chaplain. Early in his distinguished career Master Henry Bowet fulfilled this function, though he was essentially an ecclesiastical lawyer. Already Dean of Dublin, he accompanied the bishop on his Flemish crusade in 1383, and loyally gave evidence on his behalf when it ended in humiliation and disgrace.[72] Via the bishopric of Bath and Wells Bowet finally became Arch-bishop of York; and it may well be that his friendship was of crucial value to Bishop Henry in the final years when age and fortune seemed alike against him. He was not the bishop's only friend at that time,[73] and given the uncertain temperament of Henry IV one cannot entirely rule out the possibility that the fate of Archbishop Richard Scrope of York might have overtaken him had there been no voices in high places raised on his behalf. In spite of the strenuous efforts and fervent intercession of his fellow-primate Thomas Arundel, Scrope was summarily executed for his part in the Percy-inspired northern uprising of 1405, becoming, inevitably, an unofficial saint to whose tomb large numbers resorted. As for Henry Despenser he was certainly fortunate in his friends; but it could well be that it was his own gifts of friendship that called forth such friendship in others.

In later years Bowet's place as clerk or chaplain was taken by Master

William Frisby, bachelor of laws. In March 1390, he became rector of Castle Rising, having moved from the diocese of Worcester, and in a letter from Henry IV, assigned by Miss Legge to 1399-1406, he is referred to as 'your clerk William Friseby'. During the interregnum after Bishop Henry's death he acted as 'corrector-general' of the diocese.[74] It is likely, of course, that during his long episcopate Henry had other clerks and chaplains whose names have not survived, perhaps more than one at the same time.

So we move to the ordinary parish clergy of Despenser's enormous diocese. Our information about them comes largely from his register, which details thirty-four years of institutions to benefices of which, as we have seen, there were well over a thousand. Contrary to modern practice, when institutions and inductions take place in the parish church in the presence of the priest's new flock, Bishop Henry invariably carried out institutions at one or other of his manor houses, leaving the induction to be carried out by the local archdeacon or his official in the parish church at a later date. His vicars-general and commissaries generally did the same. Some clergy, no doubt, had to perform a long and arduous journey before they could track the bishop or his representative down. These expeditions could also be dangerous, as the chaplain to Lord Grey of Ruthin discovered when he was robbed while going to the bishop to be instituted, on Lord Grey's presentation, to the benefice of Mannington with Saxthorpe.[75]

We learn from the written record that the institutions took place. But under what circumstances? Any priest who has held the cure of souls in a parish knows how important it is that a bishop should relate closely, sympathetically and pastorally with a man or woman whose new charge is 'mine as well as thine'. How did Henry Despenser see his duties in this respect? Was the institution formal and rapid, or was there a real sharing of friendship and pastoral concern? After all, he might not meet the new incumbent again for a long time, if ever. Was the man properly entertained, and if necessary put up for the night? We do not know. All we have to go on is Capgrave's statement that Henry was a true pastor and beloved by all who served him. But he would hardly have written that if he had known it was far from the truth: indeed he was under no compulsion to include Bishop Despenser in his list of illustrious Henries.

The parish clergy, needless to say, differed widely. Some were highly qualified university graduates, who were often instituted by proxy. In these cases one wonders if the benefice was seen by them purely as a piece of real estate, to be served by some hired and unbeneficed priest while they took the lion's share of the income. There were, of course, many vicarages in the diocese, like the one to which John Freton retired in later life, and Bishop Henry added to these.

Vicars had security of tenure and a guaranteed, though modest, income, in return for which they promised continual residence. Alongside the university men, and at the other end of the scale, large numbers of the parish clergy were men of humble birth and attainments, like Robert of Wetheringsett in Suffolk, who was instituted to the cure of souls of his native village on 30 April, 1405.[76]

A notable feature of Despenser's register, as with others of the same period, is the number of exchanges recorded there. The latter part of the fourteenth century was the heyday of 'choppechurches', so called by Archbishop Courtenay in a strongly-worded condemnation of the practice in 1392.[77] Some of these exchanges are at first sight reasonable enough, especially those involving parishes in the neighbouring dioceses of Lincoln and London, and even more those within Norwich diocese itself. But others involve elements so unlikely and surprising that the archbishop's words are abundantly justified. Quite clearly the whole thing was a well-organised system with, in all probability, professional go-betweens in centres like London, helped by episcopal clerks in the various dioceses with a detailed knowledge of the local scene.

How otherwise does one explain the action of Thomas Barton, who in less than four months advanced himself from the deanery of Brooke to the rectory of Blickling via the rectory of St Gerrans in Cornwall? It is highly unlikely that he ever visited the West Country during this process.[78] But the swap to end all swaps occurred in 1394 between Walter Brugge and Richard Petir. This involved the rectory of Burwell, the benefice of St Patrick, Trim in the diocese of Meath in Ireland and a prebend in St David's cathedral in Wales.[79] It is noteworthy that John Thorp, licentiate in letters, acted as proctor in the transactions involving Trim and St Davids. Was he in fact the 'choppechurch broker' who arranged it all? Be this as it may, he was also the man who succeeded Robert Foulmere as Archdeacon of Suffolk in 1390.

The practice was too deep-seated and lucrative to be affected much by an archbishop's fulminations. Ambitious clerks could use it to get by stages, often quite rapid, from where they were to where they wanted to be in terms of emolument as well as place. As for Henry Despenser's register, the lengthy documents exchanged between him and outside authorities are faithfully copied out whenever an exchange takes place. They purport to say that the reasons for the exchange have been carefully investigated, but the suspicion remains that this was simply common form, which did not necessarily coincide with the facts. It is likely that the Bishop of Norwich was less worried about choppechurches than Archbishop Courtenay. Whatever other qualities he may have possessed, his mind was not conspicuously original, except perhaps in matters military. He naturally favoured the status quo, from which he had benefited well in the past. We do not, of course, know what the people in the parishes thought of all this.

But we can easily guess.

Very occasionally Bishop Henry instituted a member of a religious order to parochial work. For example, Brother John Darsham, canon of the Premonstratensian abbey of Leiston in Suffolk, was presented by the abbot and convent to the benefice of Corton and duly instituted on 16 January, 1377. But he may have been involved merely as the abbey's proctor, and not as parish priest, for on 4 February 1393, he was instituted as such to the parish of Theberton. With regular canons service in a parish was always a possibility, but that was not the case with Benedictine monks. Nevertheless, just before leaving for the Flanders crusade, the Bishop is found instituting William Shefford, monk of the cathedral priory, to the adjacent benefice of Sprowston. John of Lynn, another monk, acted as his proxy for the ceremony at the archbishop's palace at Lambeth. What lay behind that? Possibly William had not been happy at the priory, and institution to a benefice was a way of releasing him from his vows. A little later, only a few days before he set sail, the Bishop admitted a German priest, Henricus de Panstorff de Alemania, to the parish of Alderton. What, one wonders, did his new parishioners make of him?[80]

Sometimes Henry had the pleasant task of instituting priests presented by his close relatives. On 12 November 1393, Thomas, Lord Morley, a relative by marriage, presented to Monewden near Wickham Market in Suffolk. Thomas Morley appears in the register with some frequency, and is always given his title of Marshal of Ireland, a responsibility that was probably more titular than demanding. The following year it was the turn of Lady Elizabeth Despenser, his eldest brother's widow, who presented to Clopton, again in Suffolk; and on 28 April 1396, her son and his nephew, Lord Thomas, acted similarly with regard to Caldecote.

The other, unrelated Despenser family is also in evidence, for on the very same day that Lord Morley presented to Monewden Sir Philip Despenser put forward William Langton for Blakenham; and on 19 July 1398, he presented his younger son Roger to Barrow, not far from Bury St Edmunds.[81]

The scribe is indeed meticulous in describing the titles and honours of those who present to benefices. Pre-eminent among them is the king who sometimes acts by traditional right, sometimes as the guardian of a tenant-in-chief who is under age, sometimes as the de facto owner of an alien priory confiscated because of the war with France, and from 1383 to 1385 as Keeper of the Temporalities of the diocese forfeited by Bishop Henry after the ill-fated crusade in Flanders. John of Gaunt occasionally appears as patron, described as king of Castile and Leon while he was asserting that claim but as plain duke of Lancaster thereafter.[82] Considerable patronage was held by religious houses, not a little by the knightly class, and near Norwich, Yarmouth and Lynn burgesses of those places appear as patrons, presumably because they had moved into the surrounding areas and set up as country gentlemen. Sometimes, following the example of Sir Philip Despenser, they did not look far for their nominees. On 12 March 1392, Hugh Clifford, acolyte, was instituted to Haddiscoe in Norfolk at the presentation of Sir Lewis Clifford, one of the so-called Lollard Knights who made no secret of their support of the heretical teachings of John Wyclif. His theological position did not, apparently, prevent Sir Lewis from exercising his right of patronage on behalf of a relative. Another example of the same thing occurs on 19 December 1384 when young Henry Curson, who only had a clerical tonsure *(primam habens tonsuram clericalem)* became rector of Foulsham in Norfolk with the support of William and Henry Curson, the two patrons of the living for that turn.[83] He was presumably the son of one or the other.

Needless to say, Bishop Henry did not always deal with the clergy as individuals. On 17 June, 1373, at his manor of Gaywood, he issued statutes for the conduct of all clerics living in the town of Lynn. These emphasised the position of the prior of St Margaret's, a dependency of the cathedral priory, and strictly regulated the behaviour of the other clergy, particularly unbeneficed chaplains who were a sort of clerical proletariat. These had become accustomed to securing fees and offerings for themselves by officiating without permission, thereby cutting across the rights of those legally appointed to pastoral charges within the town. A special ban is placed on the holding of schools in St Margaret's and its dependent chapels, 'lest by reason of the beating and howling of the children the divine office should be interrupted and the people's devotion speedily lose its fervour'. One suspects that the bishop, while quite prepared to be a disciplinarian, might also have had a sense of humour; as for howling, Lynn was shortly to experience a great deal more of that when Margery Kempe came upon the scene.[84]

Bishop Henry was also called in to arbitrate in a dispute between the cathedral priory of Norwich and the local parish clergy. The latter were accustomed to hold a procession to the cathedral on the Sunday after the feast of the Blessed Trinity, the cathedral's patronal festival. This had suffered because of disagreements among those taking part, and its performance had become so undisciplined that the cathedral sacrist asked that something should be done. Having called a conference of all concerned, the bishop issued a firm ruling as to the form the procession should take in the future, and to this the 'discreet men' who were present as assessors gave their support.[85]

Besides these specific occasions there is evidence, albeit scanty, that in Bishop Despenser's time regular synods of the clergy were held in the diocese of Norwich. In his celebrated quarrel with St Albans Abbey over Wymondham

Priory, when he asserted his right to appoint the prior of Wymondham as collector of clerical taxation, he claimed that 'the aforesaid prior owes obedience to the bishop and is obliged to attend each one of his synods'. Moreover in 1401 Arnold Pynkeny, parson of Terrington, bequeathed the fruits and revenues of his church 'from the day of my death until the synod following next Michaelmas'.[86]

As he moved round East Anglia Bishop Henry sometimes availed himself of monastic hospitality. Having no quarrel with the great Benedictine house of St Edmundsbury he occasionally put up there while working in the southernmost part of his diocese. Other monasteries that saw a good deal of him were at Ipswich and Stoke by Clare.[87] In November 1379, he visited the Augustinian canons of Flitcham and West Acre in quick succession, and much later, in November 1401, he called on their brothers at Butley and their sisters the canonesses at Campsey Ash.[88]

Sometimes he became involved in matters of monastic discipline. By 1389 the Augustinian house at Walsingham had clearly got into a very bad state in terms of discipline and financial integrity. Given its fame as a place of pilgrimage this was a serious matter. So on May 21 of that year the indispensable Sir Thomas Morley was asked to head a royal commission to investigate its affairs. At that time the priory was in the king's hands as the rightful patron, Roger Mortimer, was a minor in his custody. Other commissioners appointed by the bishop had deposed the prior, John Snoring, but he had appealed to the Holy See. On 24 October John Hertford was appointed in his place. But in June 1390, the king's commission, strengthened by the prior of the cathedral monastery and the abbot of St Benet at Holme, were ordered to make sure that none of the canons should be given any kind of responsibility, disciplinary or financial.[89] With this total absence of trust things could hardly have been worse.

After this dismal story the doings at Bungay offer light relief. It appears that a nun of the Benedictine priory there, Katherine Montacute, had left the enclosure and was wandering about various parts of the realm in secular attire. From the point of view of the Church this was a very serious matter, involving her eternal salvation, and when it became an open scandal Bishop Henry notified Edward III, who commissioned a number of local notables to have her arrested and taken back to her nunnery to be punished. This happened in March 1377, and to judge from her aristocratic name Katherine may have been a formidable lady of the kind such circles often produce. Perhaps there were two factions in conflict within the priory. What actually happened to her we do not know; but when the prioress, Elaine Declesworth, died in 1380 Katherine Montacute was appointed in her place. Had she, one wonders, experienced a dramatic amendment of life; or was it felt by the other nuns that she would make the life of any new prioress so difficult that the best thing to do was to appoint Sister Katherine herself in the hope that the responsibility would steady her? If so they seem to have reasoned well, for under her rule no further scandals occurred, and she remained as prioress until 1396 when she died and was succeeded by Margaret Smallburgh.[90]

Bishop Henry's main contact with the religious houses in his diocese was in making the appointments of their superiors. When a vacancy occurred the monks or nuns proceeded to an election, the result of which was notified to the king so that he could signify his approval. Wormegay, yet another Augustinian foundation, was a small and poor house eventually united with Pentney. On February 8 1388, Richard II informed the Bishop of Norwich that he approved the election of Hugh Fincham as prior. On 6 April following Hugh appeared before the Bishop at Hoxne for his formal institution and blessing, but Henry quashed the election, probably because there were not enough canons at the priory to make a legitimate election possible *(propter ineptitudinem materie eiusdem)*. Nevertheless, by the Bishop's special grace, the appointment was allowed to stand. Otherwise, of course, a new election would have required a fresh application for royal approval. Finally the Archdeacon of Norfolk was commissioned to install Hugh in his priory church.[91] Many elections were quashed in this way by the bishop, but as at Wormegay the convent was still allowed to have the superior it preferred. It should also be noted that superiors-elect always had to go to the bishop to receive formal appointment and blessing, even the abbots of comparatively important houses like St Benet at Holme, Langley and Sibton, which were Benedictine, Premonstratensian and Cistercian respectively.

Not surprisingly, after the dispute with Bishop Henry over Wymondham in 1380, the authorities of St Albans Abbey took care to safeguard their rights when the famous historian Thomas Walsingham was appointed prior of their daughter house of Wymondham in 1394. When he duly appeared before the bishop at South Elmham on September 15, Thomas took the oath of obedience 'saving the privileges of the monastery of Saint Alban aforesaid.'[92]

Having dealt at Lynn with the disadvantages of keeping schools in churches, Bishop Henry acted more positively with those at Thetford and Norwich. When, on 22 August 1402, he commissioned Edward Eyr as master of the grammar schools at Thetford he was continuing a history of education in that town that went back at least to the time of Herbert de Losinga. For Dean Bund, Eyr's earliest known predecessor, was in office before 1114, and is honoured to this day as the first headmaster of that ancient foundation.[93]

In the following year, 1403, it was the turn of Norwich to receive a new master in the person of Master John Hancock. Although the cathedral priory maintained a school in the almonry for a master and thirteen boys, Hancock's appointment was to the episcopal school which, not unnaturally, was in the gift of the bishop. Already rector of Alderford, Hancock treated his school as many clergy treated their benefices; he served it by deputy. One of those who took his place was Robert Welles and another John Seguard, who was removed 'for too freely reproving the monks for writing dirty verses'. Later in his career Hancock leased the episcopal grammar school to Master John Rykkes and became master of the almonry school also. Besides the original charity boys on the priory foundation the master of the almonry school was allowed to accept a further twelve fee-paying pupils; so one way and another this educational entrepreneur made himself an excellent living. Like Master Henry Well he contributed towards the finishing of the cathedral cloisters.[94]

Herbert de Losinga is traditionally considered to be the founder of the present Norwich School as well as that of Thetford; and indeed his interest in education was so great that few, if any, of his successors have surpassed him. It is unlikely, for example, that Bishop Henry had the time or the inclination to give boys personal tuition as Herbert did. But he had other ways of pushing forward promising careers. Benefices and deaneries (which, as we have seen, had no duties attached) could be, and often were, given in much the same way as scholarships and exhibitions are today. Furthermore it seems that those in a position to do so were usually keen to discover and help along boys from any background, however humble, who showed character and potential: and these in turn, when they succeeded in life, were not unmindful of the rising generation and its needs. So while there was nothing remotely like universal education in the fourteenth century, it is possible that many – perhaps most – of those who deserved their chance were given it by rich patrons, clerical or lay.

Much of the evidence for Bishop Henry's proceedings derives from his register, which has been selectively quoted. This large compilation was apparently the work of a single unknown scribe, whose identity is only gradually revealed. After twenty years, at the end of the ruling regarding the procession to Norwich Cathedral which has already been mentioned,[95] he records that Masters John Darlington and Gregory Strode were present at the enquiry, together with many witnesses. He then adds 'And I, William Ferriby, clerk of the diocese of York and notary, scribe of the acts of the venerable father in God Henry, by the grace of God Bishop of Norwich, also subscribe to the agreement set out above'.[96]

For the first sixteen years of his service in that capacity William, like many other notaries public, was a clerk simply because he had accepted the first tonsure. He had no orders, major or minor. But on 1 October 1386, Bishop

Henry instituted him to the benefice of Snitterley (the old name for Blakeney) together with the chapel of Glandford, on the presentation of the abbot and convent of Langley. This he retained until 1395, except for a short break in 1388 when he was dean successively of Heacham and Cranwich. At that time he was in deacon's orders. On 9 September 1391, he was collated to Blofield, a benefice given by the Bishop to some of his most favoured clerks, remaining its rector until February 1400, when Robert Foulmere was collated in his place.[97] From the certificate already mentioned regarding the presentation to Walsoken we learn that William was a bachelor of laws. In fact, apart from the one instance mentioned above, he gives no indication at all of any personal involvement when he writes entries concerning himself.

How did William Ferriby go about the task of keeping the bishop's register? Although Henry Despenser travelled a great deal it is highly unlikely that the register went with him. Continual loading and unloading would have damaged it, and its present condition is remarkably good. The likelihood is that it was kept in some central place, and Ferriby made notes as he travelled round with the bishop for later transcription. The danger of such a procedure is that the entries can get out of chronological order, and this is precisely what happened. Frequently he has recourse to pointing hands, initial letters and marginal notes in an attempt to set things right. On other occasions he would have us believe that Bishop Henry was in Norwich and London on successive days, or even on the same day, a schedule that today would require a car or an inter-city train to make it possible. Although Henry was a vigorous man and clearly capable of hard riding, his Jehu-like qualities would hardly have extended to that.[98]

Few people have the gift of perfect health, and sometimes there are signs that Ferriby is not at his best. He then makes mistakes. This is particularly evident in September 1402, when at folio 285R a different scribe takes over. But he did not allow the illness, or whatever it was, to keep him away for long, and soon the familiar well-formed hand returns. Even so, there is definite evidence of a decline in his powers during the final years of the register, by which time he may have been as old as his master. After 1389 there are no more artistic masterpieces as may be seen on his headings for 1378, 1382 and 1389 itself.[99]

Like John Darlington, William Ferriby was clearly a loyal and exceptionally faithful servant. It would have given him pleasure to be able to record that in August 1391, the bishop was at last quit of the £37,475 7s. 6d that had been advanced to him for the expenses of the Flemish crusade. He takes care to keep the actual acquittance, which is interleaved.[100] And we share his sadness when he writes the following to indicate that his labours of 34 years are done.[101]

'Here ends the register of institutions carried out in the time of the reverend father-in-Christ and lord Henry, bishop of Norwich of blessed memory, who died on the 23rd day of the month of August in the year of Our Lord 1406, and in the thirty-seventh year of his consecration, on whose soul may God have mercy.'

Notes

1. Register, F15V.

2. Register, F5V.

3. C. Fine R. 1367-1377, p. 118. Edward Despenser took Froissart to see it when he was staying with the family (Chronicles, vol. I, p. 148.

4. Inquisitions Post Mortem, Vol. XVII, 15-23 Richard II, 1391-1399, 1988, p. 67.

5. Le Neve, *Fasti Ecclesiae Anglicanae,* ed. Duffus Hardy, Oxford, 1854, vol. 2, p. 465.

6. *Anglia Sacra,* ed. H. Wharton, London, 1691, vol. I, p. 415.

7. C.P.R., 1367-1370, p. 459.

8. In 1371 the Bishop's officers certified to the king that there were 806 parishes in Norfolk and 515 in Suffolk. E. H. Goulbourn, *A History of the See of Norwich,* London, 1876, p. 444.

9. Before the disastrous fire of August 1st 1994, this register was lodged in the County Record Office, Norwich Central Library, with the reference DN Reg. 3, Book 6. Fortunately the register was undamaged, and is now located at the new Archive Centre, County Hall, Norwich, with the same reference. Excluding documents at the end it runs to 335 folios or 670 pages. A microfilm copy is also available under reference MF. 508.

10. R. Midmer, *English Medieval Monasteries (1066-1540),* London, 1979.

11. R. Virgoe, 'The Estates of Norwich Cathedral Priory 1101-1538' in *Norwich Cathedral, Church, City and Diocese,* London and Rio Grande, 1996, pp. 357-358.

12. H.B. Workman adds the picturesque detail that on taking possession Bishop Henry found that the doors and windows of his manors had been carried off during the interregnum. *John Wyclif,* vol. 2, pp. 64-65.

13. A delightful drawing of a rabbit and a sheep forms part of the heading for 1382 on folio 78V of the Bishop's register. The scribe was obviously a talented artist. See plate facing the title page.

14. See drawing on page 117.

15. On December 29th, 1387, during the invasion scare of the late 1380s, Bishop Henry obtained permission to crenellate this house. The same permission was given for Gaywood. It may have been felt that West Norfolk was in need of more strong points of this kind. C.P.R., 1385-1389, p. 381.

16. The direct road to London from Norwich ran via Thetford, Newmarket, Braughing, Barkway (both on the present B.1368), Ware and Waltham. The Bishop would presumably have joined this road at Newmarket when travelling from South Elmham or Hoxne. H.S. Bennett, *The Pastons and their England* (second edition), Cambridge, 1932, p. 154.

17. He did not always use it. In 1399 he stayed with his friend Robert Foulmere, and on several occasions is found at Chelsea. Register, F252R, F243V and F244R & V.

18. See below, Chapter Four.

19. Curson is still a Norfolk name; and one modern Curson, recently deceased, confirmed a link with the Billingford and Foulsham area.

20. *C.P.R.,* 1381-1385, pp. 386, 410.

21. *C.P.R.*, 1381-1385, p. 380.

22. ibid. John Cressingham had been Steward of Lynn in 1372. C.Cl.R., 1369-1374, p. 386.

23. *C.P.R.*, 1377-1381, pp. 555-556; 1385-1389, p. 184.

24. Register, FF159V, 170R (for Flixton) and 178V among many other examples. For the Official of the town of Lynn see Register, F258V and D. M. Owen, *The Making of King's Lynn,* London, 1985, pp. 133-135.

25. E. H. Carter, *Studies in Norwich Cathedral History,* Norwich, 1935, pp. 38 and 44.

26. *C.P.R.*, 1396-1399, p. 15.

27. John Capgrave, *Liber de Illustribus Henricis,* ed. F. C. Hingeston, Rolls Series, 1858, p. 170.

28. Register, FF.10V and 15V.

29. Register, F.1R. Sutton died in 1371.

30. A.B. Emden, *Biographical Register* (Oxford) vol. 1, p. 573. For his doctorate see Register, F.78R, which amends Emden.

31. For the offices of Vicar General and Official Principal see A. Hamilton-Thompson, *The English Clergy,* Oxford, 1947, pp. 46-52.

32. M. D. Legge, (ed) *Anglo-Norman Letters and Petitions,* Oxford, 1941, letter no. 75, pp. 125-127. Lord Morley was married to Anne, a daughter of the Bishop's eldest brother Edward. There is a letter of Darlington himself at no. 87, p. 135, asking for a vacant office for his clerk Robert Aylemer.

33. Dissolved in 1544. The Assembly House stands on the site.

34. 'Nient obstant que le dit Maistre J Derlyngton est un des principales del conseil mon dit reverent uncle, il serroit toudiz prestz de mettre les matires suisdites en sa parte pur bon fyn et accord avoir en arbitracion del dit Maistre J(ehan) Derlyngton'.

Regarding the condition of St. Mary-in-the-Fields: 'Et plus outre considerer le povere estat de dit Maistre J(ehan) Rykynghale et de son povere college, quelx sont en point d'estre anientisez si noun soit par le graciouse aide et confort de vostre tres honurable seignurie'.

35. F. Blomefield, *An Essay Towards a Topographical History of the County of Norfolk,* London, 1806, vol. IV, p. 172. Register, FF. 16V, 39R, 41R and 121V to 122R. Darlington became archdeacon through an exchange with Master William Swinefleet, who received Hingham and a prebend in the collegiate church of Lanchester in the diocese of Durham.

36. Register, FF.42 R & V.

37. C. Rawcliffe, *The Hospitals of Medieval Norwich, Studies in East Anglian History 2,* Norwich, 1995, pp. 105, 108-109, 119-120 and plate 7.

38. Emden, *Biographical Register* (Oxford), p. 573.

39. E. Ekwall, *The Concise Oxford Dictionary of English Place-names,* fourth edition, Oxford, 1960, p. 188.

40. A. B. Emden, *A Biographical Register of the University of Cambridge to 1500,* Cambridge, 1963, p. 296.

41. On 3rd April 1389, he instituted the new prior of Horsham St Faith: Register, FF.136V-137R.

42. Register, F.200R (19th July 1395, when Carleton was still only an acolyte) and F.272R (4th September 1401).

43. E. H. Carter, ut supra, p. 58.

44. Emden, *Biographical Register* (Cambridge) p. 244.

45. *C.P.R.*, 1370-1374, p. 425. He was a receiver of petitions to Parliament from 1376 to 1384.

46. Register, F.31V. Master Robert de Prees, the Bishop's clerk and candidate, had been instituted to the same archdeaconry on 13th March 1374 (Register, F.24V), but had been ousted by the action of certain royal servants. See the Bishop's complaint in *Rotuli Parliamentorum,* vol. 2, p. 330. For a similar example see note 49 below.

47. *C.Cl.R.*, 1374-1377, p. 545.

48. Register, F.139R.

49. Register, F.262V.

50. Ralph Selby whose appointment as Archdeacon of Norfolk in 1398 was set aside in favour of John Middleton, gave up a distinguished career as an academic and royal servant to become a monk of Westminster Abbey, where he remained until his death in 1420 (Emden, *Biographical Register,* Cambridge, p. 517). He was, however, charged with conspiracy against Henry IV in 1410, so his retirement from the world may have been only partial.

51. Register, F.258V.

52. For Rickinghall's career see Emden, *Biographical Register* (Cambridge) p. 480.

53. Register, F.304R. He was still B. CAN L. See also F.327V for a similar entry.

54. For Well's career see Emden, *Biographical Register* (Cambridge) pp. 625-626. For the gift to Norwich Cathedral Priory see: *Norwich Cathedral, 1095-1096* (ut supra), p. 173.

55. *C.P.R.,* 1385-1389, p. 14: Register, F.111V. Richard II's presentation is dated August 18th 1385, at Morpeth in Northumberland, on his way home from his abortive invasion of Scotland. Bishop Henry was with him at the time, though still deprived of his temporalities after the ill-fated crusade of 1383. One suspects a degree of collusion between king and bishop in some appointments. The two men never wavered in their friendship.

56. *C.CL.R.,* 1381-1385, pp. 368-369.

57. Register, FF.122V and 147V.

58. For Foulmere see Emden, *Biographical Register* (Cambridge), pp. 238-239. For the use of his house by the Bishop see Register, F.251R.

59. Register, FF.329R & V and 330R.

60. See below, p. 110-111.

61. *C.P.R.,* 1405-1408, pp. 213-214: Register, F.281R.

62. Register, FF.241R and 243R.

63. A. Hamilton-Thompson, op. cit., p. 67 and note 4: F. L. Cross (ed), *The Oxford Dictionary of the Christian Church,* Oxford, 1957, p. 188.

64. Register, FF.187V to 188R. No records of Despenser's visitations survive.

65. Register, FF.162V to 164R.

66. *C.P.R.,* 1388-1392, p. 470. He also subscribed to the adjudication by Archbishop Arundel in 1411.

67. *Proceeding and Ordinances of the Privy Council of England, 1386-1410,* ed. Sir Harris Nicholson, 1834, pp. 165-167.

68. Register, FF.187V and 230V.

69. M. D. Knowles, *The Religious Orders in England,* vol. 2, Cambridge, 1955, p. 375. Leicester continued to serve Bishop Despenser's successors until his death in 1424. For Smyrna see Revelation 1, v. 11; 2, vv. 8-11.

70. Register, F.247V.

71. Register, FF.258R & V: 305V.

72. Emden, *Biographical Register* (Cambridge), pp. 83-84. For the Deanery of Dublin see C.P.R., 1381-1385, p. 224.

73. See below, p. 128.

74. Register, F.145V: Legge, *Anglo-Norman Letters and Petitions,* letter 9, p. 52: I. J. Churchill, *Canterbury Administration,* London, 1933, Vol. 1, p. 204; Vol. 2, p. 78.

75. Legge, op. cit., no. 46, p. 94. This is a letter from Lord Grey to Anthony Mallory. A Leonard Mallory was the Bishop's esquire at the time of the Clippesby affair, some twelve years before the date of this letter. The

chaplain, John Scarle, was instituted on April 17th, 1404 (Register, F.306R).

76. Register, F.318R.

77. A. Hamilton-Thompson, op. cit., pp. 107-108.

78. Register, F.45V (9th June 1376) and F.47R & V (1-2 October following).

79. Register, F.191V.

80. Register, FF.49V and 171V (Darsham), 87V (Shefford), and 88R (Panstorff).

81. Register, FF.183R & V, 196R, 210R, 237R. For the other Despenser family see *Complete Peerage,* London, 1916, vol. 4, pp. 287ff.

82. He appears as king of Castile and Leon in the register on FF.61R, 70V, 111V. By F.151V the title has been dropped.

83. Register, FF.164V and 106R. For Clifford see below, p. 109-110.

84. D. M. Owen, *The Making of King's Lynn:* a documentary survey, London, 1985, no. 125, pp. 133-135. For Margery Kempe see *The Book of Margery Kempe,* translated with an introduction by B.A. Windeatt, Harmondsworth, 1985.

85. Register, F.204V.

86. Margaret Aston, *Thomas Arundel: a study of church life in the reign of Richard II,* Oxford, 1967, p. 69, quoting *Gesta Abbatum Sancti Albani,* ed. H. T. Riley (Rolls Series 1867-1869), vol. 3, pp. 128-129.

87. Register, FF.22V and 23R.

88. Register, FF.65V and 275R.

89. *C.P.R.,* 1388-1392, pp. 36 and 74.

90. *C.P.R.,* 1374-1377, p. 490: Register, FF.73R and 217 R & V.

91. *C.P.R.,* 1385-1389, p. 401: Register, F.128R. Professor Harper-Bill points out that this difficulty frequently happened at Dodnash Priory.

92. Register, F.195R. For the dispute see pp.89-90 below.

93. Register, F.284R: *900 Years: Norwich Cathedral and Diocese,* ed. J. Wilson, Norwich, 1996, p. 60.

94. Register, F.298V: R. Harries, P. Cattermole and P. Mackintosh, *A History of Norwich School,* Norwich, 1991, pp. 15-17.

95. See p.30 above.

96. Register, F.204V.

97. Register, FF.119R, 126V, 128V, 131R, 159V, 254V. For Snitterley see Ekwall, op. cit., p. 48.

98. For example F.53R (in Norwich *and* London on 6th July 1377); F.194R (5th August 1394 in London, 6th August in Norwich). On F.230R (December 1397) he is alleged to have travelled between Norwich and London in one day three times between the 6th and the 30th. He was then approaching 55 years of age.

99. Register, F.56V (dragon for 1378); F.78V (sheep and rabbit for 1382) and F.136V (pike for 1389).

100. Register, FF.158V and 159R.

101. Register, F.335R.

3. The Bishop and the Peasants

Those seeking to understand Henry Despenser – insofar as that is possible – need first to consider his thirty-six years as a diocesan bishop. It may well be that the broad outline of his episcopate, as set out in the last chapter, was not markedly different from what went on in other dioceses at the same time. But during those thirty-six years the routine pastoral work and administration took up far more of his time and effort than the unusual and exciting events that set him apart from his contemporaries and justify the use of the word 'extraordinary' to describe him.

It was the Peasants' Revolt in 1381 that first brought Henry Despenser to the centre of the stage and guaranteed his place in history.

Many attempts have been made to explain the causes of this phenomenon which turned England upside down. The present position seems to be that it came about, not so much through grinding oppression leading to despair, but because hopes arising out of better times were still unfulfilled. To use Christopher Dyer's words, 'there is now general agreement that the condition of peasants as well as wage-earners tended to improve after the plague of 1348-1349, so that any economic explanation of the revolt must be expressed in terms of rising expectations.' This being so, it is not surprising to find that leadership did not come from the most disadvantaged, but rather from those who held positions of modest authority and repute in the local communities – those whom Dyer calls 'the village élite' – together with artisans and craftsmen living in more urban areas.[1]

But even great discontent and unrest, be it with the local landowners or those running the country, needs something to set it ablaze; and in the early years of Richard II's reign taxation of unusual harshness produced the necessary flashpoint.

At that time the government was chronically short of money, and poll taxes, each heavier than the one before, were granted by Parliament in 1377, 1379 and 1380. The theory was that in any community the well-to-do should help their poor brothers and sisters; but where this did not happen the burden on the poor was excessive. Two shillings from a man and his wife was a serious matter on top of the other traditional taxes, the fifteenths, that were still being levied. Not surprisingly there was much evasion; and when the collectors were told to redouble their efforts and tighten up their scrutiny, the methods they employed were open to serious criticism and even outrage. At the same time the war with France was going badly; in fact the French were raiding the south coast of England, and the commons, not unreasonably, were angered still further by the ineptitude of the lords who were supposed to be defending them. Add to this the inflammatory and egalitarian preaching by hot-headed clergy like John Ball –'When Adam delved and Eve span, who was then the gentleman?' – and it is not surprising that south-east England, and other areas further afield, erupted into rebellion early in June 1381.

Opinions differ as to whether the outbreak was spontaneous or had some planning and organisation behind it. Suffice it to say that the Kentish rebels found an effective leader in Wat Tyler, a former soldier. Under his guidance they marched on London and soon, with collusion within the walls, entered it, doing vast damage to buildings and property alike. A number of leading people were put to death, including Simon Sudbury, Archbishop of Canterbury. Meanwhile the contingent from Essex, where many of the outrages connected with the poll tax had occurred, had marched up to Mile End and were establishing contact with their brothers from Kent.

King Richard had determined to go by boat to meet the Kentishmen at Blackheath; but their demeanour was so threatening that he was advised against it, and the royal party withdrew without achieving its purpose. Later, at Mile End, the King conceded that serfdom or villeinage should be abolished, that labour should be paid for on a basis of free contract, and that land should be rented out at fourpence an acre. He also agreed that those the commons regarded as traitors should be punished if found guilty by due process of law.

Meanwhile, on Saturday, 15 June, Bishop Henry Despenser instituted a clerk to the benefice of Fersfield near Diss. The next act recorded in his register is on July 1.[2] There is no indication that anything of importance had happened in the meantime. But in fact these were to be among the most exciting and dangerous days of a life full of incident.

For on that very day, June 15, there took place the final confrontation between Richard II and the host of rebellious peasants at Smithfield just outside London. Wat Tyler, whose behaviour was both insolent and over-confident, was killed by the Mayor of London, William Walworth, aided by an esquire named Standish; and after the king bravely put himself at the head of the insurgents, thus preventing them from attacking him when they saw their leader fall, the menace and momentum of their actions were stemmed and the authorities quickly regained control.[3]

But did Bishop Henry know anything of this when he set out from his palace at Norwich for the family manor of Burghley near Stamford, over eighty miles away?[4] The Kentish rebels had arrived at Blackheath only two days before, and the Essex contingent had assembled at Mile End the day before that,[5] so it is just possible that a messenger might have brought news of trouble in the south before his departure from Norwich. In any case his journey took

40

him through areas of Suffolk where there was already rebel activity, and only the speed with which he travelled may have helped him to avoid it. Bearing in mind that he carried out an institution before he left on the 15th (assuming that the date in the register is correct), his arrival at Burghley by the end of the following day is no mean achievement.[6]

Two questions immediately present themselves. First, why did Bishop Henry go to Burghley at all, particularly if he knew he might meet trouble? Certainly he was a courageous man who would not shrink from danger or allow rumours to deflect him from his course. But that apart, a possible answer is that one of his brothers, Sir Thomas Despenser, who was closely associated with Burghley, had died in the previous February and that in consequence there were family matters demanding Henry's attention. Since his eldest brother's death, in 1375, his episcopal rank made him head of the family. Lady Elizabeth Despenser, Edward's widow, also held lands in the same area.[7] Secondly, bearing in mind that a little later, on his return journey to Norwich, he is described as being 'armed to the teeth',[8] did he take his armour with him? There can, of course, be no certain answer to that, but if there were it would help us to estimate the amount of danger he foresaw. Presumably he did not always take his armour around with him, but if on this occasion he either wore it, which would have been tiring over a long distance, or had it carried on a pack animal, his rapid passage from Norwich to Burghley is all the more remarkable. Another possibility, albeit slight, is that he made use of his dead brother's armour, which he would have found at Burghley. Or perhaps Walsingham was embroidering still further what was already a good tale.

What is quite certain is that by the time he arrived at Burghley the whole of East Anglia was in a state of anarchy. As R.B. Dobson's detailed chronology makes clear,[9] groups of rebels were roaming at will through Suffolk, Cambridge-shire and Huntingdon and were moving into the south-western part of Norfolk. Bury St Edmunds had been occupied by a band led by John Wrawe, a rene-gade priest who was particularly violent in his methods. At Cambridge, charters and muniments belonging to the university were burned by the mob, and the masters and students were menaced by a combination of dissident burgesses and rebels from the surrounding countryside. In the continual strife between town and gown the former element found itself in a uniquely strong position. Not far away Richard Leycester led a revolt at Ely, while at Thetford the authorities were forced to pay twenty marks to another band of rebels under Geoffrey Parfreye.

Worse still, blood had been shed. Prime targets were members of the legal profession, blamed by the insurgents for documenting their servitude and denying them justice. Its most distinguished member, Chief Justice Sir John

41

Cavendish, was brutally murdered by one gang in the vicinity of Mildenhall while another ransacked his house in Bury and stole his valuable plate from Cavendish Church, where he had attempted to conceal it.[10] A justice of the peace, Edward Walsingham, was slain at Ely, while at Bury the great abbey was given over to the fury of the rebels. As there was no abbot to murder, the office being vacant, the prior, a gentle soul expert in singing and church music, suffered instead. He was joined in death by two colleagues, one of whom, John Lakenheath, was responsible for the collection of manorial dues and fines, and therefore particularly hated.

The general lawlessness and mayhem had no directing principle behind it in most areas of East Anglia. Pillage, revenge and the destruction of compromising documents were the rebels' main concern. But in Norfolk a real leader emerged. Geoffrey Litster, no peasant, but a dyer by trade, was proclaimed 'King of the Commons' by his followers. It has been suggested, as a result of recent studies, that these were in the main textile workers rather than peasants properly so called.[11] On 17 June the terrified burgesses of Norwich opened their gates to him, whereupon he held state in the castle while his supporters sacked the city. Various local knights had fallen into his hands, namely Lord Scales, Sir Thomas Morley, Sir John Brewes and Sir Stephen Hales. These were forced to perform menial services while concealing their real feelings.

Another, however, was incapable of dissimulation. Sir Robert Salle had risen from the ranks, and enjoyed a wonderful reputation as a soldier. But he was tactless, and when he told the rebels exactly what he thought of them they put him to death. Because of his humble origins they had hoped to enlist his support. According to Froissart, his murder greatly distressed all knights and gentry who heard of it; no doubt Bishop Henry shared their feelings when he eventually received the news.[12] Indeed, it would have reinforced the revulsion he already felt as a result of his knowledge of the atrocities committed during the Jacquerie, the French peasant uprising, over twenty years before.

But not all reacted in this way. Some local gentry had actually joined the rebels; the most notorious of these was Sir Roger Bacon of Baconsthorpe. Not only did he lead an attack on Great Yarmouth, but he actively supported the rebel cause in other areas. Opinions differ as to the motives of these dissident gentry. Some have suggested that their economic interests were close enough to those of the rebels to induce them to empathise and to make common cause with them. Others put it down to sheer irresponsibility, and a desire to share in the excitement and the loot. Undoubtedly the aristocracy has thrown up ne'er-do-wells of this kind in almost every period of history; and the gentleman gangster was already a feature of fourteenth-century life as he was going to be in the fifteenth.

Having arrived at Stamford, Bishop Henry was not left in peace for long. The very next day, while Geoffrey Litster and his company were being admitted into Norwich, word came that the great abbey of Peterborough was being attacked by a band of rebels made up of its tenants and other local people. Their intention was to murder the abbot, but it is reasonably certain that destruction and pillage were also on the agenda. The resources at the Bishop's disposal were pitifully few, but without hesitation he came to the rescue and inflicted condign punishment on the assailants. Some of these were killed, including a group who, having taken refuge in the abbey church, were deemed not to deserve the right of sanctuary after the crimes they had committed and had intended.[13] This was drastic action, and Henry has been criticised for killing these people out of hand; but he had caught them in the act, and sanctuary was not designed to succour those who attacked the institution that offered it.

At this point it is worth pausing to consider the situation he was in. There were no great lords in the area to give a lead. The principal landowners in East Anglia tended not to live there but on estates elsewhere. William Ufford, Earl of Suffolk, did of course have local influence, but he had taken flight, his meal half-eaten, when he heard that the rebels were on their way to enlist his support. Of all the natural leaders of the area only Henry Despenser, Bishop of Norwich, was able and willing to act. Those further down the social and administrative scale, the sheriffs, the representatives of the absent magnates, the knightly class and the gentry, were reluctant to take up a firm position. Faced by the power and insolence of the rebels, they held their hand until someone they could trust and follow came forward.[14]

So Bishop Henry and his little group of supporters were completely on their own. His responsibility was awesome. First he had to answer for the lives of those who followed him. Secondly, in order to raise the morale of the gentry and win their support, he had to display decisive qualities of leadership. And this would undoubtedly involve – as indeed it already had – the crushing of opposition and the taking of human life. This, of course, he was not authorised to do, but under the circumstances there was really no alternative. Examples had to be made to encourage his friends and sow doubt and confusion among his enemies. So Henry resolved to fight his way back to his diocese where his main responsibility lay; and one can only endorse the judgement that 'almost alone among the governing classes (he) kept his sense of proportion and his wits about him'.[15]

It will be objected that this was no way for a bishop – a man of God – to behave. But this judgement, entirely proper under twenty-first-century circumstances, does not apply to the situation in which Henry found himself. He was, of course, almost unique in that he was a trained soldier, indeed a belted knight, before the Pope plucked him from the profession of arms and made him a bishop. But in any case the idea that clergy should always be non-combatant was certainly not universally held in the fourteenth century, in spite of the prohibition of military activity by men in holy orders set out in canon law.[16]

Examples of this are not lacking. At Crécy in 1346 the new bishop of Durham, Thomas Hatfield, was one of those who rallied to the young Black Prince when he was in great danger. Later in the same year, just outside Durham itself, Archbishop Zouche of York, with John Kirkby, Bishop of Carlisle, led the English army that defeated the Scots and captured their king at the battle of Neville's Cross. Much later Thomas Hatfield contemplated joining the papal wars as Henry Despenser had already done. At home Edmund de la Beche, from a knightly family whose tombs can still be seen at Aldworth in Berkshire, was archdeacon of that county when he was appointed by Edward III to the key post of military governor of the Isle of Wight. The island, both then and later, was a frequent target for French retaliation.[17] As for the inferior clergy, they could expect to be called out as a kind of clerical Home Guard in times of national emergency.[18]

There is even evidence that young men of noble family might hesitate between a military career and the church. William Beauchamp, a younger son of the Earl of Warwick, is a case in point. He studied at Oxford from 1358 to 1361, and had already benefited from papal provisions and dispensations when he decided to follow the profession of arms instead. In this he acquired a fine reputation, fighting with the Black Prince at Najera in 1367. But his involvement in the Flanders Crusade was much less glorious, as he argued with the Bishop over pay and was widely criticised.[19]

We must not, however, assume that the two callings were mutually exclusive and incompatible. Military and spiritual considerations might well supplement each other. We are told, for instance, that Archbishop Zouche 'went forth like the good shepherd against the wolves to save his sheep from the jaws of the Scots'. Similarly it is fair to say, with John Capgrave, that Bishop Henry was equally anxious to safeguard his sheep in the diocese of Norwich from the depredations and false ideas of the rebellious peasants.[20]

Whether or not the Bishop and his party returned to Stamford after the tumult at Peterborough he was certainly on his way home by June 18. The local centre of activity had by then shifted to the great fenland abbey of Ramsey. According to the *Anonimalle Chronicle* a band of rebels tried to capture Huntingdon, but the people drove them away. They then went to Ramsey where they compelled the abbot to give them provisions. But the people of Huntingdon, together with others from the area, followed them, set upon them, killed twenty-four and put the heads of some of them on high trees as a warning to others.[21] Dobson, however, simply says that the abbot, aided by Bishop Henry, dispersed a rebel group from Ely.[22] These two accounts can be harmonised if we assume that the force attacking Huntingdon came from Ely. But what is noteworthy is the new spirit infusing the defenders of Huntingdon and the others confronting the rebels. Civic pride may have had something to do with it, but one suspects that Henry Despenser's presence and example may have been the decisive factor. At the same time his tiny force may have started to gain reinforcements.

As one negotiates, indeed survives, the frantic rush of cars and heavy goods vehicles on the modern A14 between Huntingdon and Cambridge it is not easy to think of the intrepid bishop and his supporters following much the same route to the university city on the primitive roads of that time. But by 19 June he had arrived at Cambridge, and on that and the following day order was rapidly restored.[23] For that to happen the force of his personality must have been at least equal to the military force at his disposal. John Hanchach, a gentleman of some substance and leader of the local insurgents, was delivered to the headsman, others were imprisoned, and the remainder were sent away with strict instructions never to offend again.[24] With the revolt thoroughly quelled, Bishop Henry started on the next stage of his journey back to Norwich.

Passing Newmarket his force took a route somewhat to the right of the modern A11 road as it moved towards Thetford. This brought them to the village of Icklingham, and here he had a remarkable stroke of luck. Coming in the opposite direction was a delegation from Geoffrey Litster on its way to London to obtain a charter from the king, preferably one more favourable to the insurgents than any granted already. This consisted of Litster's three principal lieutenants, Seth, Trunch and Cubitt, who had with them a large sum of money levied from the city of Norwich. With them also were Sir Thomas Morley and Sir John Brewes. The knights, presumably unarmed, were intended to act as go-betweens on arrival at the court. Meanwhile their experiences at the rebel camp had left them thoroughly cowed. There is no reason to believe that they were there voluntarily, still less enthusiastically.

Bishop Henry, who would have known the knights, ordered them on their loyalty to tell him whether there were any traitors to the king present with them. At first they did not tell the truth, for they were greatly in awe of the peasant leaders and did not think that the Bishop, 'a young and daring man' to use Walsingham's description, had asked the question seriously or was in any position to help them. Henry, however, soon convinced them that he was in earnest and they denounced their captors. Two of the rebel leaders were immediately arrested, and the third joined them when he returned from searching for food.

There is a discrepancy in the sources over what happened next. Walsingham believed that the three were put to death there and then, but Capgrave's account is the more plausible, even allowing for the fact that quite inaccurately he has Despenser coming from London and not from Stamford. Although the Bishop realised that he was not strictly permitted to take life, he had little alternative but to do so. There was the obvious possibility of escape or rescue. This necessity accepted, no advantage was to be gained from executing them in a remote place like Icklingham. It would make better sense to put them to death where their punishment would have a profound effect on supporters and opponents alike. So, according to Capgrave, the three lieutenants were taken to Wymondham, where the Bishop heard their confessions and granted them absolution before they faced the executioner.[25]

This last episode must seem well-nigh incredible to most modern minds. But in its medieval context it was not. Henry Despenser, for all his military zeal, never forgot that he was a bishop and had final responsibility for all his flock, even those who had taken up arms against lawful authority. Every soul, however stained by evil, needed to be helped on its way to God through confession and absolution, and this duty he faithfully discharged. It would also, of course, help to legitimise his actions and defend him from hostile criticism. From this time Bishop Henry's cause prospered increasingly. Success breeds more success, and the gentry, conscious that they now had a leader, rallied to his support. So far as the insurgents were concerned, it was now over a week since the death of Wat Tyler, and it is reasonable to suppose that they were aware of it. Their morale would undoubtedly have suffered, not least as they contemplated their increasing isolation.

Even so they could have made a much better showing than they eventually did. A new study by Cornford and Reid[26] reveals that Geoffrey Litster's fellowship was only one of three active in Norfolk at the time. A large group or congregation was moving about in the area of Rougham, to the north of Swaffham, where John Reed, a collector of the poll tax, was an obvious target. It seems to have had no coherent strategy apart from attacking people like Reed and John Pagrave, a local farmer and justice of the peace. Eventually, so far as one can see, it simply broke up and dispersed. Had it instead moved north-east and joined up with Litster, Bishop Henry would have faced a more formidable adversary. The third group came from Lynn, where a large group of artisans, always a volatile element as the Bishop already knew to his cost, rose in revolt.[27] These attacked places in the vicinity of Lynn, including Snettisham, East Rudham and Castle Rising, but it is far from certain whether they even knew what was going on elsewhere.

From Wymondham the Bishop's forces, now augmented, marched the last few miles to Norwich, which he entered on Monday, June 24.[28] Here, besides a vastly relieved populace, he found abundant signs of looting and wilful damage. He also learned that Reginald Eccles, another justice of the peace, had been put to death by the rebels.

Henry Despenser did not stay for long in Norwich. He lost no time in following up Geoffrey Litster and the main body of rebels who had withdrawn to the area of North Walsham. The *Anonimalle Chronicle* states that he wrote letters to the commons warning them to desist from their wrongdoing and return home.[29] But events were now moving so quickly that it is unlikely that they had much effect, if indeed they were written at all. Litster had a house at Felmingham, just to the west of North Walsham, and it is likely that this part of north Norfolk was the epicentre of his part of the revolt. In the time left to him he worked energetically to stir up the country against what he called the 'bishop's tyranny', visiting, among other places, Thorpe Market and Gimingham, between North Walsham and the coast.[30]

For his part, according to Capgrave, Bishop Henry had decided, in the spirit of Caiaphas, that it was better that one man should die rather than all perish.[31] If this can be taken at face value, it confirms that his policy was to make an example of leaders, while sparing the remainder and allowing them to return home with a warning as to their future conduct.

So the scene was set for the final confrontation. A battered cross, and the remains of two others, mark out an area to the south of North Walsham, adjacent to the B1150 road to Norwich, where the battle that ended the Peasants' Revolt in Norfolk took place. To help defend themselves, Litster and his men had created a fortified enclosure out of carts and other impedimenta, not dissimilar, perhaps, to those employed centuries later by wagon trains in the Wild West when confronted by Indian war parties.

Bishop Henry, with his military training, would not have underestimated the opposition. We do not know if Litster himself had any experience of warfare; but others in his company would very likely have seen service against the French. There may have been expert bowmen among them, particularly effective when shooting from cover; and one is again reminded that the anger of the rebels extended to more than the poll tax and the insensitive way in which it was collected. Those with experience in past campaigns particularly resented the ineptitude with which the war was being conducted. Not only was the tax unjust, but those entrusted with the proceeds for national defence were failing in their duty. The fact that the French, by a sensible change of tactics, had made victory all but impossible had not escaped the indignant commons with their memories of Crécy and Poitiers, where the enemy had contributed to their own downfall.

47

But those commons would have been surprised to learn that Bishop Henry, to judge from his actions before and during the Flanders Crusade, largely agreed with their poor opinion of the military leaders of the time.

But here at North Walsham the insurgents had done the best they could, and their position could only be carried by direct assault. It is impossible that Bishop Henry would have allowed anyone else to lead it, and with his little army he plunged into the fray.

What happened then is difficult to assess. Walsingham speaks of a pitched battle in which the Bishop acquitted himself gallantly, while the French historian Reville records a local folk-memory referring to large numbers of dead. Capgrave, on the other hand, infers that after the initial assault the commons quickly gave up, rejoicing because they were allowed to go away peacefully and without further punishment.

A quite different fate awaited Geoffrey Litster, 'the idol of Norfolk'. Trying to escape by hiding in a cornfield he was betrayed and sentenced to be beheaded. Yet here again, as at Wymondham, Henry did not forget that he was the condemned man's bishop. Confession was made and absolution given; and then, acting with remarkable consideration and compassion, Henry walked beside his adversary to the place of execution, bending down to prevent his head from being jarred on the rough ground as he was dragged along. Here was a man who had risen against his king, committing and condoning many crimes in the process. But Bishop Henry clearly saw in him a worthy foe, and in doing so showed a humanity and a chivalry that up to now he has been almost universally denied. We can, I believe, accept that this was not one of Walsingham's purple passages. Its very unexpectedness carries the ring of truth.

Nevertheless the extreme punishment took its grisly course. Of Litster's four quarters three were sent to Norwich, Yarmouth and Lynn. The remaining one was exhibited outside his house 'so that rebels, and those who rise against the peace, may learn how they will end'.[32]

After this success, modest as it was, the Bishop of Norwich enjoyed an enviable reputation as a soldier and man of action. But not all were prepared to submit. Rumblings of discontent continued for some time, and his name appears on commissions to put down rebellion in Rutland, Suffolk and Norfolk.[33] In the following year a plot was organised to murder the Bishop and other people of importance at the great fair of Horsham St Faith. The conspirators then proposed to capture the abbey of St Benet at Holme to serve as a base for future activities. But one of their number betrayed them, and they were tried and beheaded at Norwich.[34]

As for Henry's own irregular actions in executing rebel leaders, he was pardoned, with others who had overstepped the mark, by the Parliament that met at Westminster in November, 1381.[35] The roll of this Parliament also gives a list of seventeen people from Norfolk who were to be exempted from pardon.

Some, however, saw the revolt as an opportunity for paying off old scores, and appear to have made false accusations of complicity. John de Spayne, of Bishop's Lynn, was accused, among other things, of being a chief captain in the great insurrection by hostile people in the hundreds of Galhowe and Brothercros. His name, in fact, is on the list just mentioned, where he is described as a 'cordewaner'. But Bishop Henry testified to his in-nocence, and he received a royal pardon. One wonders if his apparently foreign origins may have had something to do with the accusations levelled against him.[36]

More surprising is Bishop Henry's involvement in an incident far away in Kent. It appears that certain pilgrims from the northern counties on their way to Canterbury had spread the story that John of Gaunt had freed the bondmen on his estates. This had a disturbing effect on some men from the Maidstone area, who had probably been involved in the 1381 uprising. Led by one Thomas Hardyng, they had started a movement to compel the king to grant them the liberties conceded at Mile End and subsequently withdrawn. Moreover they proposed to send messengers to John of Gaunt to establish the truth of what they had heard from the pilgrims. If it were so, they were prepared to make him king in place of his nephew.

Remains of one of the crosses erected on the battlefield at North Walsham

One can be pretty sure that this affair was no more than a storm in a teacup, and feelings towards the hapless rustics who had been thus stirred up should, perhaps, incline towards pity. But they did make some sort of gesture, and the authorities, very much on their guard, took it seriously and arrested them all. At this point John Cote, a mason from Loose, just to the south of Maidstone, turned king's evidence[37] and received a pardon for his felony and treason at the supplication of the Bishop of Norwich. Cote, one suspects, was not a very pleasant person, for he accused William atte Welle of Loose and

49

other people unnamed of felony, though they were all subsequently acquitted. He was not worthy, perhaps, of the episcopal backing he received; and in any case, how did Bishop Henry get to hear of him?[38]

It has been mentioned already that the Bishop erected three crosses to mark the site of the battle of North Walsham. It is generally agreed that the magnificent retable, or altarpiece, in St Luke's Chapel at Norwich Cathedral (usually known as the Despenser Retable) was given as a thank-offering for that victory. It was provided, either by the Bishop in person or by several donors, including him, who were involved in the suppression of the rebellion. It depicts the Passion, Crucifixion, Resurrection and Ascension of Our Lord, and is one of the finest examples of late fourteenth-century art to be found anywhere. Among the coats of arms that embellish it (some have been lost) are those of Sir Stephen Hales, one of Litster's prisoners and servitors, and Sir Thomas Morieux, who took an active part in restoring order in Suffolk. Needless to say Despenser's arms are there too, described heraldically as 'quarterly argent and gules, the second and third quarters fretty or, and over all a band sable'. Round this ancestral coat Henry placed a blue (azure) border charged with the golden mitres of his episcopal arms. Other representations of this shield are to be found at St Margaret, King's Lynn and on the outer east wall of the church of St Andrew in the city of Norwich. It is also the coat of arms of Viscount Falmouth, of Tregothnan in Cornwall, who is the 26th Lord Le Despenser.[39]

Almost a hundred years ago learned controversy centred on whether the Despenser Retable was painted by English or Italian artists. Modern experts are much less ready with theories and conclusions. As David King points out, 'the only conclusion to be drawn is that there was such a variety of stylistic experiment and influence in the second half of the fourteenth century, and so much comparable material has been lost, that it is impossible to make categorical statements concerning the provenance of this work based on style alone'.[40]

What can be suggested is that Bishop Henry had an interest in art, and that this interest, soon to be demonstrated again, was aroused by his years in Italy fighting in the papal wars. To those wars, albeit in a very different setting, he was shortly to return.

Notes

1. R.H. Hilton and T.H. Aston (ed), *The English Rising of 1381*, Cambridge, 1984, p. 41.
2. Register, FF.74V and 75R.
3. For the account of the Peasants' Revolt I have drawn on M. McKisack, *The Fourteenth Century*, Oxford, 1959, pp. 406-419.

The Despenser Retable in St Luke's Chapel, Norwich Cathedral

51

4. *Dictionary of National Biography,* vol. 14, pp. 410-412.

5. McKisack, op. cit., pp. 408-409.

6. H.S. Bennett, writing about the fifteenth century, concludes that those needing to ride fast could cover between 35 and 40 miles daily at almost any time of the year. In extraordinary circumstances, given good weather and good going, 50 miles a day was not impossible. *The Pastons and their England,* Cambridge, 1968 edition, pp. 158-159.

7. *Inquisitions Post Mortem,* vol. 15 (1-7 Richard II), H.M.S.O., 1970, pp. 138-139.

8. *'armatus ad unguem'* Thomas Walsingham, *Historia Anglicana,* ed. H.T. Riley, Rolls Series, 1863-1864, vol. 2, p. 6.

9. R.B. Dobson, *The Peasants' Revolt of 1381,* 1970, pp. 41-43.

10. For a full account of the revolt in East Anglia see McKisack, op. cit., pp. 415-418.

11. Dobson, op. cit., Introduction, p. XXVI.

12. Froissart gives a highly-coloured account of his death, in which he kills numerous rebels before being slain himself *(Chronicles,* ed. Geoffrey Brereton, Harmondsworth, 1968, pp. 222-224). By contrast the *Anonimalle Chronicle* calls him a great robber *(grant laroun)* as well as a hardy and vigorous knight. There is no support for this contention anywhere else, though of course he may have served with the Free Companies. *(The Anonimalle Chronicle 1333-1381,* ed. V. H. Galbraith, Manchester, 1927, p. 151.)

13. *Chronicon Henrici Knighton.......Monachi Leycestrensis,* ed. J. R. Lumby, Rolls Series, 1895, vol. 2, p. 140.

14. For this section I am indebted to R.H. Hilton and T.H. Aston, op. cit., pp. 194-212.

15. Ibid, p. 194. John Capgrave contrasts the Bishop's courage with the cowardice of the nobility *(Liber de Illustribus Henricis,* ed. F. C. Hingeston, Rolls Series, 1858, p. 170.).

16. See F. L. Cross (ed), *The Oxford Dictionary of the Christian Church,* Oxford, 1957, pp. 1438-1439, quoting *Codex Iuris Canonici,* canon 141. Although 'military' bishops were a rarity in England they were quite common in Italy: R. Brentano: *Two Churches: England and Italy in the Thirteenth Century,* Los Angeles, 1968. I am indebted to Professor Harper-Bill for this reference.

17. B. Croucher, *Village in the Valley: A History of Ramsbury,* Ramsbury, 1986, p. 40. De la Beche was Prebendary of Ramsbury in Salisbury Cathedral.

18. For example they were called out soon after the death of Edward III. The French were expected to take advantage of the minority of Richard II by attacking the south coast of England. C.CL.R., 1377-1381, p. 88. For Thomas Hatfield see Margaret Aston, 'The Impeachment of Bishop Despenser', in *Bulletin of the Institute of Historical Research,* XXXVIII, no. 98, November, 1965, pp. 131-132.

19. W.M. Ormrod, *The Reign of Edward III,* Yale University Press, 1990, p. 132: A. B. Emden, *Biographical Register* (Oxford), vol. 1, pp. 138-139. For Beauchamp's part in the Flanders Crusade see Walsingham, *Historia Anglicana,* vol. 2, p. 94.

20. Antonia Gransden, *Historical Writing in England,* London, 1982, vol. 2, p. 17, quoting *The Lanercost Chronicle,* p. 347. The pastoral aspect of Bishop Henry's action during the Peasants' Revolt is emphasised by Capgrave, op. cit., p. 172.

21. *The Anonimalle Chronicle,* p. 150.

22. Dobson, op. cit., p. 42. *The Anonimalle Chronicle* mentions the part played by William Wightman, a minor Chancery official, in organising the successful resistance.

23. Capgrave, op. cit., p. 170.

24. Dobson, op. cit., p. 42: Capgrave, op. cit., p. 170.

25. For the events at Icklingham and Wymondham see Walsingham, *Historia Anglicana,* vol. 2, pp.6-7:

Capgrave, op. cit., pp. 171-172.

26. B. Cornford and A. Reid, *The Uprising of 1381* in *An Historical Atlas of Norfolk,* Norwich, 1993, pp. 86-87 (including map).

27. See below, pp. 83-87.

28. Dobson, op. cit., p. 43.

29. *The Anonimalle Chronicle,* p. 151.

30. Capgrave, op. cit., p. 172.

31. St John's Gospel, chapter 11, verse 50.

32. For the final events of Bishop Henry's campaign see Walsingham, op. cit., vol. 2, pp. 7-8: A. Reville, *Le Soulevement des Travailleurs d'Angleterre,* ed. C. Petit Dutaillis, 1898, p. 139.: Capgrave op. cit., p. 172.

33. *C.P.R.,* 1381-1385, pp. 245, 247, 248.

34. Walsingham, op. cit., vol. 2, p. 70.

35. *Rotuli Parliamentorum,* vol. 3, pp. 98ff.

36. *C.P.R.,* 1381-1385, p. 272.

37. The medieval equivalent was 'urn approver'.

38. For the whole incident see *C.P.R.,* 1381-1385, pp. 237 and 264-265.

39. The latest discussion of the retable, with full references to earlier work, is in David King's article in *Norwich Cathedral, Church, City and Diocese,* Norwich, 1996, especially pages 410-413. The same book has an illustration of Bishop Henry's private seal (page 453, fig. 169). Suitably martial in character, it shows his coat of arms below a mantled helm surmounted by a mitre. This in turn supports a large crest of a silver griffin's head. Also shown are the arms of his see and those of his mother, Anne, daughter of William Lord Ferrers of Groby.

40. King, op. cit., p 413.

The seal of Henry Despenser, Bishop of Norwich

4. The Crusading Bishop 1380-1383

Part One: Preliminaries

When Urban V consecrated Henry Despenser as Bishop of Norwich in 1370 he may well have been alive to the possibility of using a man with dual qualifications, albeit an unusual combination, should a situation calling for both of them arise. Urban died soon afterwards; but in the time of the next pope to bear that name the moment seemed to have come. Undoubtedly Henry himself thought so, and acted accordingly.

In the year 1378 the Great Schism in the papacy began; it would last until 1417. Urban VI established himself in Rome, while Clement VII resided at Avignon in the south of France. Ever since 1305, long before the schism began, the papacy had been settled in Avignon in what has been called its Babylonish Captivity. The reasons for the schism lie outside the scope of this study; suffice it to say that the countries of Europe aligned themselves behind one or other of the rival pontiffs while they hurled abuse and anathemas at each other. England followed Urban; France adhered to Clement; and therefore a religious split paralleled and exacerbated the state of war already existing between the two countries. From now on both sides could see their enemies as schismatics as well as foes, and the possibility of proceeding against them as such was quickly raised.

It may be thought that the crusading spirit had expired with the final expulsion of Christian forces from the Holy Land in 1291. But this was far from being so. The Teutonic Knights were still campaigning against the heathen in Prussia, Poland and the lands adjacent to the Baltic Sea. Many knights and esquires from other parts of Europe, England included, made their way to those regions to seek adventure and gain military experience. Not only that: the genuine flowering of chivalry that was a notable feature of the fourteenth century led many to look towards the Holy Places and long to regain them for the true faith.[1] At the very end of that century a prolonged truce between England and France permitted knights from both countries to enlist together in a crusade that ended disastrously at the battle of Nicopolis in 1396. In that battle the French showed the same ill-considered impetuosity that had lost them Crécy in 1346, and was to cause the disaster of Agincourt less than twenty years later.

Everyone knew where they stood with the Saracens who controlled the Holy Places. But could a crusade be legitimately proclaimed against Christians who were schismatic, that is to say supporters of the pope you did not recognise? Events soon answered this question in the affirmative. It is, of course, easy – and cynical – to point to the attractiveness of a crusade against people with whom you are at war anyway. But earlier this century the great French historian Edouard Perroy strongly disagreed with other scholars who denied the sincerity of those who crusaded under such circumstances.[2] But the circumstances could change, as we shall see, and the crusaders' motivation could change with them.

Bishop Henry made his first move early in 1380. In February of that year his clerk Henry Bowet, later to be Archbishop of York, went to Rome on a diplomatic mission from King Richard II. He was also given instructions by his episcopal master to raise the question of a crusade against the supporters of Clement VII.

Urban VI was more than ready to respond to this initiative, and on 23 and 25 March, 1381, two bulls were issued to recognise Bowet's endeavours and to set preparations for a crusade in motion. The first, *'Dudum cum vinea Dei'* (Recently the vineyard of God), recalls the condemnation of Clement VII and gives a crusading indulgence to all those who, during the year after a date to be fixed by the Bishop, would take part in an expedition against the schismatics or would contribute towards its success by substantial donations. The second, *'Dudum cum filii Belial'* (Recently the sons of Belial), gave the Bishop of Norwich power to allow any clerk, exempt or not exempt, regular or secular, to take the cross without the agreement of his superiors, and to dispense them from restrictions regarding residence. It will be noticed, however, that neither of these bulls specifically appointed Bishop Henry as leader of the future crusade, though the fact that they were issued to him implied it. He was, in fact, left free either to conduct the expedition in person or give the command to a lay captain of his choice. Nothing was said as to where, or against whom, the crusade should be launched, and not surprisingly the English authorities pressed hard for clarification on this point.[3]

Before Bishop Henry could publish the bulls and proceed further the Peasants' Revolt broke out, and he had to assume a military role of a very different nature. When it ended, his position was considerably enhanced. Apart from malcontents among the peasants and craftsmen, he was regarded as something of a hero; as such, a future assignment as leader of a crusade would be more readily accepted in spite of his episcopal status. However, his success at North Walsham was really a temptation to over-confidence. We do not know to what extent, if at all, he had held independent command in the Italian wars; but the comparatively easy conquest of a peasant uprising was scant preparation for the rigours of a campaign overseas. An assessment of his actual performance must wait until later.

Early in August 1382, Bishop Henry received a third papal bull, which had been promulgated on 15 May. *'Dignum Censemus'* (We consider it fitting) required him to preach against the schismatics in the provinces of Canterbury, York and Cashel in Ireland. He was to pursue all rebels against Pope Urban, should any exist in England and its possessions, deprive them of their dignities and give them to those who were worthy. Those he arrested were to be imprisoned and sent to the curia in Rome under suitable escort.[4]

Everything was now ready for the preaching of the crusade. Having assumed the title of Papal Nuncio, the Bishop named his clerk Henry Bowet as his commissary general. Then, on 17 September, he sent copies of the three bulls to the other diocesan bishops with orders to publish them.[5] But while these preparations for a crusade were going forward, events of a very different nature were taking place, and these were to shape quite radically the course the crusade itself would eventually take.

During the later Middle Ages the trade in wool between England and Flanders was so important that Flanders, to quote Perroy, was like a prolongation of England on the Continent.[6] The route the exports took was carefully worked out and suited all concerned. First it crossed to Calais, the Staple through which all wool had to pass. Then, after English taxes had been paid, the wool was taken to Bruges, the great commercial and banking centre of Flanders, and then on to the principal weaving towns like Ghent and Ypres where it was finally made up into cloth.

While this system was firmly in place English interests prospered, particularly those of the great London merchants and entrepreneurs who controlled the Staple at Calais. But should the political situation in Flanders become unstable the worst consequences were to be feared; and this is precisely what happened. A period of strife between Louis de Mâle, Count of Flanders, and the conflicting authorities of Bruges and Ghent ended with the latter city in firm control of the area under the rule of a popular leader, Philip van Artevelde. Artevelde was no friend of France or of England; he was only concerned with Ghent and Flanders. Consequently the orderly traffic in wool from Calais ceased; and when the English government, thoroughly alarmed, entered into negotiations with him he demanded that the Staple should be transferred, first to Bruges for a transitional period of three years, and then to another town in Flanders which Ghent would have the right to choose. Dire as they were, these events were overtaken by another worse still. In November 1382, a large French army invaded Flanders, and on the 27th defeated and killed Van Artevelde at the battle of Rosebeke. Two days later Charles VI of France and the Duke of Burgundy entered Bruges in triumph, and at once banned all commercial relations with England.[7]

Indeed, things could not have been worse. But what, if anything, could the English government do? How could it export its wool to the Continent and prevent the trade from collapsing altogether, with all the suffering that would entail among its subjects? The people of Ghent, now deprived of their leader, looked desperately to England for support. How could it help? It was possible to re-route some of the wool so that it arrived in Zealand, further to the north, where the French were not in control. But the only realistic course of action seemed to be an armed invasion of Flanders to expel the French and re-assert English interests there, together with those of her traditional trading partners.

But who should lead it? At first there was a strong feeling that the king should do so himself; but eventually the view prevailed that the times were not suitable for him or his uncles to leave the country, particularly in view of the possibility of a Scottish invasion. But these objections did not apply to the Bishop of Norwich. More and more support was given to his idea of a crusade against the schismatic French, which would first attack them in their new power-base in Flanders and then, should things prosper, go on to invade France itself. This of course would have the added, but hardly spiritual, effect of rescuing the wool trade in alliance with Ghent, which was in any case the only effective support England had against France in the area. Furthermore a crusade, as distinct from a normal military operation, could be financed from ecclesiastical sources and so reduce the strain on an Exchequer continuously short of money. This was particularly urgent as both Parliament and the clergy had been very reluctant to allow taxation since the time of the Peasants' Revolt. As a plan it seemed almost too good to be true. The only objection – not, in the event, taken seriously – was that the Flemings, unlike the French, were in fact supporters of Urban VI. Therefore it was surely wrong to unleash a crusade against their country in his name.

A heavy burden of responsibility lay on the royal Council and also on Parliament when it met on 1 October 1382 and again in the following February. To summarise some tortuous negotiations and impassioned proceedings, Parliament found that two hats – or rather a hat and a mitre – were now in the ring. For John of Gaunt, Duke of Lancaster, was also making a 'proffer' to counter that of Bishop Henry. Through his wife he had a claim to the throne of Castile and Léon in Spain, a claim which is, as we have seen, fully acknowledged in the Bishop's register. These lands, like France, adhered to the cause of Clement VII at Avignon. He therefore argued that an invasion of Spain would not only support his claim to the Castilian throne, but would also embarrass the arch-schismatics of France on their vulnerable southern flank.

Not surprisingly the Lords in Parliament and the aristocracy in general were on the side of Gaunt, who was generally respected though rarely popular. The idea of an expedition led by a churchman, even one with noble blood and a royal kinsman, seemed deeply discreditable to the natural leaders of the country. They also raised understandable doubts about the Bishop's competence to undertake such a heavy responsibility alone.

But the Commons thought differently. Particularly after the battle of Rosebeke their over-riding concern was the future of the wool trade with Flanders. To save this, and the very livelihoods of many of them, a speedy and effective invasion of Flanders was imperative. So the 'Way of Flanders' gained ground over the 'Way of Spain', and by the beginning of the second session of Parliament in February 1383, Bishop Henry was so confident of success that he ignored a summons to consult with the Council beforehand and only appeared in time for Parliament itself.[8] In this instance he was justified, though hardly wise, for the 'Way of Flanders' did in fact prevail. John of Gaunt did not help his cause by a characteristic display of petulance and an angry withdrawal from Parliament.

Serious negotiations regarding the details of the expedition could now proceed. Eventually it was agreed that it should consist of 2,500 men-at-arms and 2,500 archers. Bishop Henry was to serve the king for a complete year, and 2,000 of the troops were to proceed as quickly as possible to the aid of Ghent. Should the French change their allegiance and accept Urban VI before the stipulated year was up, he would abandon the crusading element of the expedition, fold up his special banner, and complete his engagement by fighting them under the usual military conditions.[9]

So far, so good. But the worry that existed about his own leadership persisted. Quite apart from those who felt that a bishop should not fight under any circumstances, others who did not share these scruples felt it unsuitable that a prelate should deal with disciplinary functions more suited to a secular leader. In reply Henry submitted four names of suitable leaders from whom the king might choose a lieutenant. One of these, Sir John Neville, was considered but it was felt that there would be so many differences between him and the Bishop that the crusade would be fatally compromised. In fact Henry put up so many obstacles that eventually, while still holding to their view about a lieutenant, the Council left the vital loophole which allowed him to assume total leadership if he thought fit to do so. This, of course, was what he had wanted all along; but it would leave him in a very weak position should the crusade go badly wrong.

Very careful preparations had already been made for the crusade. Bishop Henry would have had knowledge of earlier crusades and their shortcomings, and was therefore opposed to taking along large numbers of enthusiasts unskilled in war, not to mention women whose presence, for obvious reasons, would undermine morale.[10] In the second of these laudable aims he was successful; in the first he was not, with all the unfortunate consequences he had foreseen.

Apart from the actual invasion of Flanders and the logistics associated with it, the Bishop faced two heavy adminstrative problems. These were the provision of money and the raising of the agreed number of troops. For finance he had three sources available. Regarding the first, his own pocket, his original 'proffer', or proposal to Parliament, stated that he would himself meet the costs of shipping and all other necessary charges.[11] Certainly his self-confidence would have led him to commit as much as he could spare. As for public funds we have reasonably precise information as to what he received. From the fifteenth Parliament had granted for the crusade, Robert Foulmere, the Bishop's receiver, was given £29,000 from the Exchequer on 17 March 1383, while a further £3,004 10s. 5d went to John Philpot, the distinguished London merchant whom Henry had appointed treasurer of the expedition.[12] On May 9 Philpot received a further £6,266 13s. 4d, making in all £38,271 3s. 9d.[13] Much later, on 16 and 22 July, additional sums of £100 and £892 15s. 1d were paid over to Philpot to meet the cost of sending reinforcements.[14] These sums, however, do not correspond with the £37,475 7s. 6d of which Bishop Henry was finally acquitted by the Exchequer in August 1391.[15]

But it was not at all the intention that taxation should meet the whole of the burden. The great attraction of a crusade, whether one prefers to put the word between inverted commas or not, was that much of the funding should be provided through the Church itself. Here the Bishop's planning was particularly detailed. Having already sent to the dioceses copies of the papal bulls giving him authority, he next appointed commissioners to act in each one. These were to recruit and oversee the preachers and confessors who were to proclaim the crusade and who, with their attendant clerks, were allowed to keep sixpence of every pound they collected.[16] As many of them were friars this windfall would be more than welcome.

When the deputation arrived in a parish the priest was summoned and ordered to co-operate under threat of excommunication. In addition two or three of the most prominent parishioners might be invited to encourage their neighbours. Having assembled the faithful, the preachers explained the aims of the crusade and emphasised the spiritual benefits available in the form of indulgences to all who were prepared to help. These were indeed highly attractive. After due confession of sins a plenary indulgence *(plena remissio peccatorum)* would be granted to all who were prepared to go with the Bishop, either at their own expense or subsidised by someone else, in just the same way as if they were going to the Holy Land. Even if they died on the way and never saw action the indulgence would still apply, and all their sins would be remitted.

Those giving financial support, either to a named individual or in a more general way, would also receive the indulgence, even if they would not be taking part themselves. But the indulgence would not take effect until any substitute was approved by the commissioners as suitable to join the army. It could also be lost if the volunteer behaved disgracefully while on service, in which case he would be discharged with ignominy. Bishop Henry was to be told of all who were helping financially, even those whose contribution was like that of the poor widow in the Gospel,[17] so that they would not fail to obtain the appropriate spiritual blessing. He particularly wanted to know of anyone who was not co-operating, or was actively working against the crusade in any way. These were to be cited to appear before him at St Paul's in London, where they would be duly dealt with.[18]

The writer of the *Eulogium Historiarum*, admittedly a hostile source, alleges that the Bishop's emissaries went much further in their search for funds. 'They promised' he says 'indulgence to the living, and also stood on the graves of the dead and absolved them too, ordering the Archangel Michael to deliver their souls to heaven. Thus they collected a great deal of money.'[19]

On the other hand, while such proceedings are not likely to have worried the Bishop, whose theological views seem to have been thoroughly con-ventional, they predictably infuriated John Wyclif.[20] Still hurt by his condem-nation at the Blackfriars Council in 1382, he was outraged at the prospect of Christian fighting Christian, particularly on behalf of a corrupt Curia and a pope who had proved unworthy of the hopes the reformers had entertained of him when his pontificate began. The extensive use of friars as preachers of the crusade also upset and angered him. Although they had once been his allies they deserted him when he proclaimed his unorthodox views on the Eucharist, and became his most determined opponents at Oxford. Henceforth they were 'the Pope's whelps'.[21] Those who sided with Wyclif joined in the condemnation enthusiastically. John Aston, one of his leading supporters, is known to have preached a sermon against the crusade at Gloucester on 21 September 1383. Another, William Swinderby, otherwise known as 'the hermit', was to attack it in a defence submitted to ecclesiastical judges appointed by the Bishop of Here-ford on 3 October 1391. William Northwold, of whom we shall hear again, also fulminated against it at Northampton; and the recantation of Master John Cor-ringham, later to be the soul of orthodoxy and first Registrar of the Order of the Garter, contains two heterodox conclusions highly critical of the crusade.[22]

But however principled his criticisms Wyclif was entirely out of touch with the spirit of the age. Once they got used to the novel idea of a crusade the people were so enthusiastic that there would have been little need for the coercive side of the Bishop's money-raising schemes; though Walsingham was

60

probably exaggerating when he said that virtually nobody could be found in the entire country who was not prepared either to go or to contribute.[23] Genuine crusading zeal there undoubtedly was, fuelled by the offer of generous indulgences. But there was more to it than that. Here at last was the chance to put behind them the frustrations engendered by many years of military failure and confront the ancient enemy with every assurance of divine blessing. Women as well as men shared in this enthusiasm, and Henry Knighton describes how jewels and trinkets of every description showered into the Bishop's coffers. One lady offered the enormous sum of £100. 'Thus', Knighton comments, 'the secret treasure of the kingdom, which was in the hands of women, came to be consumed.'[24] For his part Froissart claimed that a large Gascon tun, which usually contained wine, had been filled with money from the diocese of London, and estimated the total receipts at 25,000 francs.[25]

There was also significant activity outside England. In the Duchy of Guienne Bishop Henry commissioned Richard Cradok, Esq, son of the mayor of Bordeaux, to pursue the cause of the crusade among the people of that region.[26] In Ireland some responsibility appears to have been given to John Karlel, Chancellor of Dublin, and his brother William. John was later called to account for irregularities in his stewardship, and did not help his case by his violent reaction when he received a citation from the papal Curia. He snatched it from the messenger, threw it to the ground, and stamped on it.[27]

To what extent did Bishop Despenser himself help to create this enthusiasm? There are many instances of how easily people become attached to a young and charismatic leader, whether politician or bishop. In 1383 Henry was still only forty, and his energy in promoting the crusade, plus his achievements during the Peasants' Revolt, may well have added further attraction to a very positive and ebullient personality. Given the extensive powers the Pope had granted him over his fellow diocesans and other clergy, the other bishops might well have regarded him with jaundiced eye; but there is no evidence that they did so, which is all the more remarkable when Henry's lack of tact, at least in his earlier days, is taken into account. If, however, the enthusiasm of the ladies had something to do with him personally this should not be over-estimated. Few would actually have seen him, and it is noteworthy that whatever his shortcomings no breath of scandal ever attached itself to his name. We have seen that his brother Edward had outstanding social gifts; and it may well be that Henry matched him in this as in many other respects.

Alongside the supply of money came the raising of men. When a man-at-arms volunteered his services, the local commissioner was to record his name, and extract from him a promise that he would enter into an indenture with Bishop Henry. Eventually, though we do not know how, he would find his proper place as the army assembled. It was also important to check the motives of those who came forward. Again and again the royal protection granted to individuals joining the crusade was revoked because they were in fact fleeing from their creditors, or were trying to escape lawsuits started against them, or had even been excommunicated.[28] Others took the Bishop's money and then absconded, while another group, non-combatants this time, gave out that they were proctors of the Bishop and, armed with forged letters, fraudulently received money for the crusade which they then misappropriated.[29]

Recent research by Colin Paine has shown that no less than 48 crusaders had links with the royal court. More surprisingly a considerable number of men associated with John of Gaunt came forward in spite of their master's well-known opposition to the crusade and its leader. When geographical distribution is considered, more crusaders came from London than from all the East Anglian counties put together, while those living north and west of a line joining the Severn and the Humber were easily outnumbered by those from the area to the south and east of it. Personal knowledge of Bishop Henry's qualities caused many to enlist, not least the knights and esquires who in 1381 had been with him on royal commissions in Norfolk and Lincolnshire. Others, again, particularly the impoverished younger sons of knightly families, offered their services in the hope of gaining military experience, and plenty of cash to go with it.

It is clear that many of the clergy, both secular and regular, took full advantange of the chance the Pope had given them to become crusaders, to the disgust of at least one monastic writer.[30] For example seven monks from St Albans Abbey and its cells joined the expedition. One of them, the prior of Hatfield Peverel in Essex, died on active service while the rest, although they returned, never regained their former health after their experiences in Flanders, having suffered from the hot weather and contaminated water.[31] Thomas Walsingham may have gathered eyewitness accounts of the crusade from one or more of these. But, sympathetic though he is, he still permits himself an ironic comment on the feelings of those clergy. When they found themselves in deadly peril confronting the enemy, did they perhaps see their former routine way of life in a more favourable light?[32]

Enthusiasts, clerical and lay, had their places in the Bishop's plan. But the bulk of his army would need to be more professional. So, inevitably, he turned to captains who would make indentures with him for themselves and a stated number of followers, both archers and men-at-arms. As he had set himself against working with the higher nobility these captains were knights banneret or ordinary knights bachelor, though a few more noble names do appear, for example William, Lord Hilton, Sir Henry Ferrers and Sir William Beauchamp. Walsingham, singles out four for special mention. First comes Sir Hugh

Calveley, an honourable man with vast experience in war, who longed to fight in a crusade before he finally retired. Next we hear of Sir William Faringdon. To his credit he was ready to speak out for the crusade, even in the presence of John of Gaunt, thus winning over many of the magnates. But later, as the chronicler remarks, he fell away badly and proved false. Other leaders mentioned are Sir William Elmham and Sir Thomas Trivet, though unfortunately at this point Walsingham decides that the full list of names would take up too much space and suppresses it.[33]

In engaging these professionals Despenser was stirring up trouble for himself, though he could hardly have done otherwise. Some, like Calveley, behaved honourably throughout, but others, including Faringdon in spite of his enthusiasm, probably saw their part in the crusade as a matter of business rather than spiritual commitment. They and their retinues were ready to serve for the proper pay, but were unwilling to take what they would regard as unreasonable risks. So while things were going well, and there were ransoms and plunder to be had, they would be perfectly content. But if difficulties emerged, they would concentrate on self-preservation; and if money was offered to them, even by the enemy, they would be unlikely to turn it down. They were more than mercenaries but not very much, as Bishop Henry was to discover to his cost when they proved thoroughly insubordinate.

Towards the end of 1382 the preparations intensified. On 21 December Henry solemnly took the cross at St Paul's Cathedral at a service conducted by Robert Braybrooke, Bishop of London. At the same time a cross was erected at the entrance to the quire of that church, perhaps to show that it had been designated as a recruiting centre for would-be crusaders. Further support came from William Courtenay, Archbishop of Canterbury, who wrote as follows: 'The Church cannot have peace without the realm, nor can the well-being of the realm be secured except through the Church, and it is both meritorious to fight for the faith, and fitting to fight for one's Lord.'

Ordinary people, too, were able to play their part by attending specially-arranged masses, sermons and vigils, for which they could receive further indulgences. The spiritual aspect of the preparations culminated on 7 April 1383, when Bishop Henry was given a crusading banner in Westminster Abbey. He then led a procession to St Paul's, where a solemn mass was sung before he left London to embark at Sandwich.[34]

More secular preparations also proceeded steadily. By putting his seal to an indenture with the King, Henry ensured that the army he led would be a royal army; and for his part Richard issued instructions which were essential to help forward the launching of the crusade. Of prime importance was the provision of a fleet to transport the army, so orders were sent out to have the necessary ships impressed.[35] Here again, such was the enthusiasm of the royal officials that some ships had to be derequisitioned because they were engaged in other important voyages or were not even English.[36] Even so, the masters of six vessels laden with supplies for the castle and town of Cherbourg were ordered, on 26 March, to have them back at Sandwich before 8 April to be ready for the passage of the crusading army.[37] It is estimated that 120 vessels eventually took part, but this did not include small boats called doggers which were rejected because they were unsuitable for the transport of horses.[38]

Bishop Henry's own movements can be reconstructed from his register. He did not return to his diocese after leaving it midway through February to attend Parliament in London.[39] Towards the end of March he seems to have moved from his own house at Charing to Lambeth Palace, probably so that he could keep in close touch with the Archbishop.[40] His next move, on or before 26 April, was to Northbourne, to the east of Canterbury, where, according to Walsingham, he stayed at a manor house belonging to the abbot of St Augustine in that city.[41] Finally, by 8 June, he was at Sandwich, where he placed his diocese in the trustworthy hands of John Darlington the Vicar-General. At the same time he issued controversial instructions regarding the affairs of the cathedral priory at Norwich, to which we shall return later.[42]

But by this time the crusade was seriously behind schedule. A large proportion of the 5,000 troops he had agreed to take had simply not arrived. Already, on 17 March, sheriffs throughout England had been ordered to proclaim that all persons due to go on the expedition were to make their way to Sandwich with all speed. At the same time the sheriffs were sent writs of aid in favour of those still collecting money.[43] On 8 April another royal mandate required these collectors to bring all the money they had to Sandwich within ten days, as the Bishop would shortly be setting out. They were also to produce the names of all who had been unwilling to contribute, so that they could be proceeded against in chancery.[44] Then, on 27 April, an even more peremptory order was sent to the mayor and sheriffs of London. Immediately they saw it they were to proclaim that all men-at-arms and archers retained to go with the Bishop should join him, ready to embark by the following Friday at the very latest. None was to remain in the city or its suburbs, and all found there after the appointed day were to be arrested and imprisoned until it was decided what to do with them.[45]

But still the army was far from complete. Then, to make things even worse, the King sent a message to the Bishop recalling him to London for consultations. This placed Henry in an extremely difficult position. It looked as if Richard intended to cancel the entire expedition, in which case all his detailed preparations would go for nothing. He may have suspected, as one modern writer certainly does, that Michael de la Pole, Chancellor of England and counsellor and governor to the King was influencing Richard against the crusade and in favour of peace with France.[46] But in any case the recall landed him in an insoluble conflict of loyalties between his King and the Pope. In such an extremity Henry's basic character might be expected to govern his behaviour, and so it did. As a man of action he loathed indecisiveness and muddle, and it was probably this that impelled him to ensure that the crusade would go ahead in the only way possible. He disregarded the order and set sail. But it was no blatant defiance. On the contrary he sought to excuse himself, explaining to the King that any further delay would be disastrous to the success of the whole venture.

So, on 16 May, the crusading army finally left Sandwich, its ships escorted by a flotilla belonging to Ghent which had evaded the French and was under the command of Francis Ackermann. Ackermann's experience and advice were to be very helpful to Bishop Henry during the earlier part of the campaign.[47] The following day the fleet dropped anchor at Calais and the great enterprise began.

It did so, however, without the participation of Sir William Beauchamp, Sir Thomas Trivet and their respective companies. Beauchamp, who had once been destined for the priesthood, was at loggerheads with the Bishop over pay, and therefore remained at home amid the curses of the ordinary people. Trivet was also very dilatory, and made no move until the Londoners and the Bishop's friends threatened him with death. Eventually he and his troops crossed to Flanders but, comments Walsingham, his coming was of no help to the Bishop, 'as will be understood from what happened next.'[48]

Part Two: In Flanders

Having arrived safely at Calais, Bishop Henry and his crusaders faced important decisions from the very beginning. Should they lose no time and attack the French schismatics in their homeland? If so, an advance towards Artois, and particularly the town of Arras, was indicated. On the other hand, was it not of prime importance to revive the wool trade by re-opening the trading route between Calais and Bruges and, at the same time, join hands with beleaguered Ghent? After all, Henry's proffer had been accepted because it was the 'Way of Flanders'. So economics prevailed over religion, and the army set out eastwards, keeping the North sea coast to its left.

This move soon brought it to the port of Gravelines, which was assaulted on 19 May. Having contemptuously refused a summons to surrender, the French garrison put up a stubborn fight but was eventually overcome. According to the laws of war then prevailing the defenders were put to the

65

sword, though the women and children were spared. The victors then found themselves in possession of considerable spoil. Three large ships were captured, together with two barges, two galleys and sixteen small fishing boats. Two hundred barrels of wine also fell into crusading hands, together with salted meat, grain and iron. So many horses were found that the mobility of the army was considerably increased.[49]

Thus heartened, the army proceeded along the coast to Dunkirk, which was occupied without difficulty on 24 May. Next day, however, the first serious opposition appeared in the form of an army estimated at about 30,000 men, made up of Flemish, French and Breton contingents brought together by Louis de Mâle, Count of Flanders. Immediately the crusaders sallied out to meet them, but before the battle began they were treated to a rousing speech by the veteran Sir Hugh Calveley which, although it may be apocryphal, is certainly worth quoting.

'Would you ever have believed', he said, 'that a town like Gravelines, well fortified and well garrisoned, could have been taken by so few? They had so many war machines, and so many defenders, that we would never have pulled it off unless God had been helping us and His hand had done it. Just think of the situation now. Here we aren't up against stone walls, with a ditch and earthworks, as we were at Gravelines. This battle will be a lot easier, for all we have to face are Flemings, who aren't used to war, and schismatics and enemies of the cross into the bargain. They have never had experience of fighting against the English. You'll see them off without any trouble at all.'[50]

For all that he was mistaken about the Flemings being schismatic (he may not have known otherwise) Calveley was only too accurate in his estimate of their experience and fighting qualities. When they moved to the attack they met the dreaded longbow for the first time. The arrow-storm, we are told, darkened the sky, and anyone who dared to look up at once became a casualty. Having put the Flemings, whose worth they also distrusted, in the front of the battle the much smaller number of French and Bretons quickly fled, and the defeat soon turned into a rout. Further help, it is asserted, was given to the crusaders by a heavy thunderstorm, which was taken to be proof of divine approval.[51]

According to Walsingham, no less than 12,000 of the enemy were killed with hardly any casualties among the crusaders.[52] These figures, if accurate, could be interpreted in different ways. Those in favour of the crusade rejoiced at the success of English arms. But those who disapproved pointed to the unpardonable evil of Christians slaughtering other Christians in such great numbers.

Such a complete victory had an immediate effect on the surrounding communities. The leading men of Bourbourg, somewhat inland from Gravelines, had already made submission, and a number of other towns followed their example. Among them were Nieuport, Bray, Fernes (Veurne), Bergues, Dixmude and Poperinghe. Parties of crusaders may have penetrated as far as Blankenberg, within easy reach of Bruges itself. To all appearances the opening phase of the campaign had been a resounding success, and having won his second battle Bishop Henry waited at Dunkirk for the reinforcements he hoped to receive.[53]

Even so there was no lack of activity. Henry's desire for independence of action did not extend to keeping the authorities at home in the dark as to what was going on. A letter in Latin still survives in which the writer describes events up to and including the battle at Dunkirk on 25 May. Mr Pantin thinks that this is the work of a monk of Westminster reporting back to his abbot, but it could equally be Bishop Henry, or someone writing on his behalf, giving the latest news to William Courtenay, Archbishop of Canterbury.[54]

In the opposite direction letters were coming to the Bishop from the government, keeping up the pressure on him to accept a secular lieutenant. At a later stage in the campaign the Earl of Arundel's name was put forward, and although Henry had no personal objection to him (indeed he was happy to serve with him a few years later), and Arundel was prepared to come with a retinue at his own cost, he raised so many reservations and objections that again nothing happened. This deliberate obfuscation was later to cost him dear.[55]

Excitement and joy marked the arrival of the good news in England; and shortly afterwards it was confirmed by soldiers who had, in defiance of their engagements, returned with plunder they had acquired at Gravelines and Dunkirk. In view of this success the government authorised Bishop Henry to negotiate with Louis de Mâle and the municipal leaders of the Flemish towns.[56] At the same time large numbers of men of military age clamoured to take the cross, among them many London apprentices who set out without their masters' permission. Clad in a modified form of crusader garb, and with inadequate arms or none at all, they presented themselves at the docks and requested passage to Flanders.[57] Sir John Philpot, who was in charge of transport arrangements, gave way to their entreaties and let them go. This, as events turned out, was most unwise. The Bishop would welcome properly trained reinforcements, but not a disorganised rabble.

Meanwhile Henry and his advisers were discussing what to do next to follow up their success. It would seem that at this point the differences that were going to ruin the entire expedition first made themselves felt. Henry, conscious of the crusading aspect of the enterprise, favoured an immediate invasion of France, and it is likely that Calveley, with a similar motivation, agreed with him. But the other captains, probably supported by Francis Ackermann, were more concerned with the re-opening of the wool trade with the great Flemish cities, of which Ypres was Louis de Mâle's last stronghold in West Flanders. Substantial help from Ghent would be available if they decided to besiege Ypres, and these arguments carried the day.

But whether they realised it or not, in so doing they were running a tremendous risk. If Ypres were to be subdued it must be done quickly or the impetus of the operation would be lost, for the crusading army was not adequately equipped for siege warfare.[58] Furthermore, the people of Ypres were solidly Urbanist and could legitimately asked why they were being attacked. The answer appeared to be that it was in the interests of Ghent, a rival city, and this stirred them to such fierce and effective resistance that the whole crusading enterprise was put in jeopardy. With the benefit of hindsight the decision to besiege Ypres was a fatal mistake.

From the time the siege began on 9 June things began to go wrong. The men of Ghent, reputedly 30,000 of them,[59] were far more diligent than the English, who were reluctant to expose themselves to danger, hoping that the town would eventually be given up without bloodshed. Realising this, the citizens of Ypres, who were well provisioned, improved their defences further and resisted more strongly still.

Then a further problem appeared in the shape of the enthusiasts who had rushed to take the cross when they heard the initial good news. Walsingham's statement that there were 60,000 of them is surely an exaggeration[60] but whatever the exact figure they were of no value militarily, and to feed them strained the Bishop's commissariat to breaking point. In fact he told them in no uncertain terms that they were more trouble than they were worth. To prevent any repetition of this he wrote to Philpot commanding him to send no one in future who was not fit for active service.

It is, however, fair to say that Henry could have had more reinforcements of seasoned troops had he not been so inflexible over the matter of leadership. But the initiative was now passing out of his hands. Dysentery made its appearance, men began to desert and return to England and, as Walsingham remarks, the condition of the besiegers became far worse than that of the besieged. It was believed that Sir Thomas Trivet, who had at last arrived, was in communication with the enemy and was receiving money from them. All Bishop Henry could do was to exhort his troops to pursue the siege more energetically before too many gave up and went home.[61] Like many other generals he was discovering the hard way that those involved in static warfare are more difficult to motivate than those with the stimulus of a war of movement.

News now arrived that a French army was on its way to relieve Ypres. Nominally under the command of the young king Charles VI, it was led by

Philip, Duke of Burgundy, husband of Louis de Mâle's daughter and heiress, who was understandably alarmed about the fate of his future inheritance.[62] When they heard of this it would have been clear to the besiegers, who up to then had been reluctant to make an all-out assault, that time was no longer on their side. The defenders had already agreed to surrender on 20 August if not relieved, but now the crusading leaders did not think that they could wait that long.

So on August 10 the besieging armies began the assault.[63] The defenders met them with stones, javelins and arrows, together with Greek fire and 'missiles which are called guns'. To scale the walls the Bishop's engineers had constructed an ingenious bridge, but one of the opposing guns scored a direct hit and it collapsed, killing the soldiers who were on it. Before long it became obvious that Ypres would not fall, and on the same evening the siege was raised. Not surprisingly the men of Ghent cursed the perfidy of their English allies and Walsingham, agreeing with them, comments that if the crusading leaders had been as faithful as those from Ghent, there would be no Ypres remaining. The withdrawal of the English army was so rapid that much equipment was destroyed to prevent it from falling into enemy hands, including several large guns worth a great deal of money.[64]

What were the crusaders to do next? Again Bishop Henry and Sir Hugh Calveley spoke up for an invasion of France and a confrontation with its army. For his part Henry felt remorse at the time that had been lost in front of Ypres, and the neglect of what he felt to be the true object of the crusade. It seems likely that Calveley had already spent time away from the siege in command of a raiding party in the direction of Arras.[65] But Trivet, Elmham, Faringdon and the other captains would not listen. They considered a confrontation with the French to be madness in view of their small numbers, and refused to obey their leader. Instead they and their forces made their way back to Bourbourg, which they fortified against the French in the expectation that they would soon arrive.

But was it madness to confront the French? For those most concerned about their own skins it certainly was; but there were precedents (even in the days before Agincourt) to show that small English armies, well led and with plenty of expert bowmen, could face and overcome French forces considerably larger, particularly if these did not have the benefit of good generals. It is not always realised that when the French army eventually went into action it also performed very indifferently, many of the soldiers being bourgeois unused to war.[66] After the captains had deserted, Bishop Henry and Calveley went into Picardy with a small force. There they encountered part of the French army and approached it with banners displayed, offering combat. But the French, we are informed, refused to fight.[67] In view of this it is not unreasonable to suggest that if the entire English army had been present, and able to bring the French to battle, a memorable victory might have been achieved; though any effect it might have had on the schism is altogether a different matter.

So the Bishop and Calvely returned to Gravelines, and in due course the French army arrived in the area. First it laid siege to Bourbourg and the captains and their retinues within it. Evidently quarrels among leaders were not the preserve of the English side, for when the Duke of Brittany advised against an assault Charles VI accused him of favouring the English, presumably on the grounds that he was married to the half-sister of Richard II, Matilda Holland. Stung by this insult the Duke insisted on leading his Bretons to the attack, but as the French looked on, his assault was repulsed and his banner captured. When their turn came the French did no better. They lost 500 men, including the Constable of France, and many, among them the Lord of Clisson, were wounded. English casualties were light, but much damage was done to the town through the besiegers' use of Greek fire.[68]

More recriminations among the French leadership followed. The King was anxious to keep up the attack, but the Duke of Brittany disagreed. The army, he pointed out, had taken many casualties to add to the large numbers lost through sickness. If things became much worse the Bishop from Gravelines might join up with the garrison of Bourbourg and cause them grave embarrassment. The campaigning season was almost over and the sooner hostilities ended the better. So it was decided that the Duke should negotiate a surrender with the English captains as he was already known to them. This stratagem proved successful, and money prevailed where force of arms could not. The English were allowed to leave the town with their horses, their arms and all their servants, together with anything else they wanted to take, and were given safe-conduct to go where they would.

Where they actually went is disputed. Walsingham states that they made for Calais with a large quantity of spoil which the French soldiers begrudged them; but Perroy believes that they rejoined Bishop Henry at Gravelines. Walsingham is more likely to be correct as the surrender terms at Bourbourg – even if they allowed the defenders to go where they wished – would hardly have permitted them to march off elsewhere and start fighting all over again. For his part the *Westminster Chronicler* confirms that the captains agreed not to carry arms against France until after they had returned to England.[69] In any case the bad feeling between the Bishop and the captains would not have made them very welcome at Gravelines; and what is more one forms the strong impression that they had no intention of fighting any further.

Next the French army marched the short distance to Gravelines and set about besieging it. Again terms of surrender were proposed, as its leaders had no wish to risk further casualties against a defending force led by such determined soldiers as Bishop Henry and Sir Hugh Calveley. According to Walsingham the terms were that the town should be levelled, and after receiving 15,000 marks the Bishop and his men should be allowed to go wherever they pleased.[70] But here again Perroy offers a different version.[71] According to him the captains, now at Gravelines, accepted bribes and the retreat of the army to Calais was arranged for 10,000 francs. Bishop Henry was kept in ignorance of this, and he was also unaware that Robert Foulmere, his treasurer, had pocketed a further 5,000 francs. When he learned of this the Bishop was extremely angry and ordered Foulmere to return the bribe to the French; but as his purse was empty the treasurer used part of it to buy provisions and hung on to the rest. Foulmere's misdeeds are certainly authentic, for they were brought up against him when the Bishop was impeached in the following year. He was then committed to prison until he should disgorge the balance of the 5,000 francs which he still had with him.[72]

But to return to Walsingham's account of events, it is clear that Bishop Henry refused the surrender terms offered to him. He had, he said, taken Gravelines by force of arms and it belonged to him, and through him to the King of England. So he was granted a truce so that he could consult Richard. This he did, explaining the difficult situation but saying that there was enough time for a relief expedition to be sent out. With its help he could still put the French to flight.

Richard received this message at Daventry in Northamptonshire, where he had been staying in the priory after a succession of other visits at monastic expense. These, incidentally, included one to Norwich where, in the absence of the Bishop, he and his queen viewed the ceiling of imperial eagles that Henry had ordered to be painted in her honour, and which still exists in the Great Hospital of St Helen, formerly dedicated to St Giles.[73] On receipt of the bad news Richard was at last stung into activity. Leaping up from the dinner table he rushed off through the night towards London, frequently changing horses.

At St Albans he borrowed a palfrey belonging to Abbot Thomas de la Mare which he failed to return. Having arrived in London he went to sleep but, on awakening, his resolve to confront Charles VI in person had evaporated to such an extent that he now talked of sending others to chase the French away. In the end, predictably, he did nothing at all. Walsingham relieves his feelings with a quotation from Horace:

'The mountains bring forth - and a silly mouse is born.'[74]

Now Bishop Henry's predicament was known, what could be done to save the situation? About 24 August John of Gaunt and his brother Thomas of Woodstock began to assemble a relief expedition on the Kentish coast, and informed the King of what they were doing.[75] But in spite of Despenser's entreaties the expedition never sailed, and perhaps the biggest question raised by the whole enterprise is, quite simply, why not?

Two explanations have been put forward. One is that Gaunt, having had his plans for a Spanish expedition thwarted by Despenser, had no intention of helping the Bishop in his hour of need. The other, probably equally valid, suggests that Richard's royal uncles were getting tired of facing responsibilities that the King himself was now old enough to confront, and Charles VI, his contemporary, was facing already.

It is generally considered, on the basis of his conduct at Smithfield during the Peasants' Revolt, that Richard did not lack personal courage. Many of his later actions, or rather failures to act, might suggest otherwise. He appears to have been unmilitary if not actually cowardly, and one can sympathise with his uncles in their reluctance to have the responsibility thrust upon them. Richard's conception of kingship appears to have been strong in the areas of ceremonial and the outward trapping of majesty; but unlike Edward I, Edward III, his supplanter Henry IV, Henry V, Edward IV and Richard III, he was unwilling to accept its rougher and less pleasant aspects. Kings who could not lead an army and share its hardships were little esteemed in the harsh world of the fourteenth century; and this may well have been one of the factors that led to his deposition sixteen years later. Even today public opinion approves of monarchs who are prepared to face hardship as an integral part of their duties. So Bishop Henry was left with no alternative but to surrender Gravelines, after having thoroughly destroyed it. His honour – a quality not much in evidence during this campaign – did not allow him to accept the 15,000 marks the French had offered; and with the faithful Calveley and his other followers he sadly made his way back to Calais, crossing to England early in October. Soon after landing he had a confrontation with John of Gaunt, in which he presumably asked why no help had been forthcoming from England. The only reply he received from the Duke was harsh and outspoken condemnation, before being sent away in disgrace. More helpfully Gaunt was successful in negotiating a truce with the French, and in this diplomacy the interests of long-suffering Ghent were not neglected.[76]

But well before any of these developments, news that the crusade was in trouble was already current in the streets of London. As early as 24 July Hugh de la Pole, a Welshman, was arrested by the city authorities for begging, and also for making out that he had been wounded at the siege of Ypres. Not content with that, he was telling everyone he met of the quarrels that had broken out between Bishop Henry and his captains. Pole was put into the pillory as a liar, which seems rather hard on him. Of begging he was guilty; of pretending to be wounded he was also presumably guilty. But in retailing the dissension and bad feeling that ruined the crusade he was speaking nothing but the truth.[77]

Part Three: Impeachment and Aftermath

Failure is a bitter pill for anyone to swallow; but given Henry Despenser's positive and masterful character he would have found it galling in the extreme. He was not even able to go home and recuperate, for Parliament was about to meet and his recent conduct would be under the closest scrutiny. In the event he was not to see Norwich again until just before Christmas.[78]

When Parliament opened on 26 October 1383 he was confronted by his accusers. These denounced him and demanded his impeachment.[79] Impeachment was the method used to call to account people who, while not considered guilty of treason, had nevertheless in official eyes done considerable harm to their country and its interests. Foremost among Henry's opponents was Michael de la Pole, no relation to the Hugh just mentioned but Earl of Suffolk, who was probably behind the attempt to call off the crusade before it left England. As Chancellor his political programme favoured peace with France, and he had already shown his hand well over a month before. On 12 September John of Gaunt was given all the powers that had previously belonged to Bishop Henry in Flanders, his instructions being to negotiate a settlement.[80] In this, as we have seen, he was successful.

De la Pole could look for support from the lords of Parliament, most of whom had backed Gaunt's 'Way of Spain' rather than Despenser's 'Way of Flanders'. As for the Commons, who had been his leading partisans, the crusade had not achieved what it was meant to achieve in respect of the restoration of the wool trade, and the Bishop could expect little sympathy from them. In any case, and most unusually, they were allowed no part in the impeachment proceedings, which were entirely a matter for the Lords. To all intents and purposes Henry was entirely on his own.

Proceedings began with the examination of his clerks Henry Bowet and Robert Foulmere, who were questioned about money alleged to have been received from the French for the evacuation of Gravelines. Bishop Henry was then formally impeached on four counts. The first two alleged that although he had agreed to serve the King with 2,500 men at arms and the same number of archers, he had not been able to collect those numbers or have them properly mustered at Calais.[81] Furthermore, having contracted to serve for a whole year, his forces had returned to England and been disbanded within less than six months. The other charges had to do with the Bishop's own leadership. First he was accused of sharp practice in refusing to divulge the names of his subordinate captains until he had been given permission to mount the expedition. In this way, his accusers said, the King's uncles and other leading magnates were effectively debarred from taking part. Also, and predictably, he was interrogated over his failure to appoint a secular lord to share command of the expedition and be responsible for military affairs and discipline.

Henry defended himself vigorously. He asserted that by the time it arrived at Ypres the army was well up to - indeed above - the agreed numbers. He considered his captains to be good and sufficient, though if the King had accepted Lord Neville's offer to go on the crusade he would have been served even better. On the question of a lieutenant there was much contention. Here, of course, Henry was in a weak position for he had certainly used every means he knew to keep the crusade under his exclusive command. On the other hand the authorities had not objected to him taking command himself under certain circumstances, so he was, at least technically, justified in so doing.

It must have been difficult for Henry to defend himself at all, for it seems that he was interrupted and heckled continuously. When he complained of this, saying that because of the conduct of his opponents he had forgotten a large part of what he wanted to say, he was given another day on which he could continue his defence in a more peaceable atmosphere. On this occasion he went back on what he had said earlier about the suitability of his captains. Had it not been for their refusal to co-operate he would have attacked the French army when it approached. Moreover, during the final stages of the retreat, the surrender by those captains of various forts (including, presumably, Bourbourg) had placed him in an extremely difficult position. He had to contend with the problem of six or seven thousand evacuated men making trouble on the beaches near Calais for lack of provisions and leadership; and only by a speedy retreat from Gravelines with the remainder of his forces was he able to rescue them and prevent their slaughter by the French. As the truce that had been arranged was about to expire, this was a distinct possibility.[82]

Whatever the arguments Bishop Henry was able to muster, his condemnation was a foregone conclusion. His temporalities were declared forfeit. No longer was the temporal sword to be carried before him, and he was to pay all the sums which had been spent on his needs out of the francs received from the French.[83] The last point seems particularly unfair, as he had steadfastly refused to accept any French bribes, and had roundly condemned Robert Foulmere for doing so.

It was also alleged that if the Bishop had been treated as a secular lord, rather than as a prelate of England, it would have been no more than he deserved in view of the secular way in which he had behaved.[84] The writer of the *Eulogium Historarium* goes even further when he says that the King ordered the Bishop to recite the entire psalter for the souls of those he had killed.[85] Of this there is no other evidence, and it seems highly unlikely, for Richard is said to have sympathised with Henry after his sentence, a kindly attitude which ensured his unswerving loyalty in the future.[86] Perhaps there was also an element of bad conscience in Richard's gesture. Should he have been in Flanders in the Bishop's place instead of visiting his cathedral?

As Margaret Aston explains there are points in these accusations with which one can easily quarrel. For example Despenser is charged with taking part in military activities unsuited to the office of a bishop. But no one in authority had seen anything amiss when he dealt effectively with the Norfolk element of the Peasants' Revolt. And Henry was by no means the only ecclesiastic to be involved in warfare during the fourteenth century, though he was certainly unique in that he had considerable experience already before Urban raised him to the episcopate.[87] Furthermore it can at least be argued that his military acumen was superior to that of his captains when he ordered an attack on the French army, particularly in view of its shortcomings which were to be revealed before Bourbourg. It might have helped Henry's cause considerably if the Lords had summoned Calveley and asked his highly professional opinion; but nobody, apparently, thought of doing so or thought it expedient to hear from the Bishop's most loyal colleague.

Even more unfair was the contention that Henry should not have given up Gravelines, as John of Gaunt was about to cross over with a relief expedition, and supplies of food were available whenever he wanted them. According to De la Pole the King had written to the bishop 'that he had appointed his uncle of Spain to come quickly to your aid and support'.[88] But even if that was what the King wanted, and the government assumed was going to happen, it did *not* happen because Gaunt, for reasons best known to himself, refused to move.

It is also undeniably true that the Bishop of Norwich was a convenient scapegoat, having already set himself up for that role as we have seen. But the conduct of warfare has always been, at least in part, a matter of good luck or bad. The story goes that Napoleon was told by a colleague of the outstanding qualities of a certain general. 'Yes,' replied Napoleon, 'but is he lucky?' During the Peasants' Revolt Despenser was undoubtedly lucky, though it can be argued that sometimes enterprise brings good luck with it. But in Flanders his luck ran out, to a large extent because of the insubordination and treachery of his captains, with the honourable exception of Calveley. Yet here again one might say that he asked for trouble by not appointing a secular lieutenant with disciplinary powers. Someone like Arundel, by threatening trial and summary execution, might have brought those captains into line very quickly. Henry, as a bishop, was hardly in a position to do that.

But the captains did not escape the condemnation they deserved – far from it. They avoided execution, it is true, but not imprisonment, and they were compelled to hand over the whole of the money they had gained so dishonourably. Sir William Elmham was forced to return two sums of 1,400 and 3,400 francs which he had received illegally from the French, together with smaller sums that had come to him as a royal admiral.[89] Sir William Faringdon and Sir Thomas Trivet had to answer for 1,400 francs each, Robert Fitz Rauf for 400 francs, and Sir Henry Ferrers, whose misdeeds are not recorded elsewhere, for no less than 6,400.[90] Robert Foulmere's punishment has already been mentioned.

In the long run an even worse punishment, was imposed upon them by Thomas Walsingham, who bitterly lamented the decline of chivalry in England.

'Alas, O Land, which formerly produced men respected by all at home and who inspired fear abroad. It now spews up effeminate men, objects of ridicule among the enemy, and of common talk among their fellow-citizens.'[91] Later he speaks of knights of the royal court who are 'more valiant in bed than in battle, better armed with words than the lance'.[92] But there is one shining exception. Sir Hugh Calveley 'was always, even in the direst straits, the most faithful comrade and loyal companion.'

As for Sir Thomas Trivet, the chronicler records his death at Cambridge, after a fall from his horse caused by using his spurs too vigorously. He gets scant sympathy, and received none from the populace, who hated him and were delighted to witness his end. Not only had he proved false to Bishop Henry, but he supported the court party against the Lords Appellant, who were seeking reform, and urged that they should be killed.[93] Had he not died thus, he might have met a much more horrible end, as some of the courtiers did when the Appellants gained control soon afterwards.

Henry Bowet, unlike those knightly miscreants, emerged with his reputation intact and continued to build the career that led him at last to the archbishopric of York. During the impeachment proceedings he had spoken up loyally for his master, recalling the dramatic scene when Faringdon came to the Bishop at Gravelines with a bribe of 5,000 francs in bags carried by two servants. Henry refused to have anything to do with it, saying that he would have no peace of mind until he knew that the money had been returned to the French in full. However much money they were prepared to send him he would never act dishonourably and risk being disgraced in the presence of his king. But Faringdon and the servants departed leaving the money lying on a table, after which Bowet told Foulmere to look after it. So it was fitting that on 13 July 1384 the Chancellor and Treasurer of Ireland were told to continue to allow him all the fruits of his deanery of Dublin as fully as if he were in residence, setting aside a statute to the effect that non-resident clergy should pay two-thirds of their emoluments towards the cost of the war, which was, as usual, endemic in that country. He had given good service both to the King and to the Bishop of Norwich at the court of Rome, and was continuing to do so, while special mention was made of his contribution to the crusade in Flanders.[94]

Needless to say, we hear nothing of the shortcomings of the King and of his mighty uncle, though in any assessment they should surely stand in the dock with all the rest. Eventually Bishop Henry was able to make his way home; but when he got there he was most reluctant to leave Norwich for a considerable time afterwards. His register reveals that in 1384 he was there from 6 January to 27 March, and again from 13 April to 6 July, though a commission to John Darlington, and institutions by him on 9 and 18 May, suggest that he may have been away for a short period. He was in London (but not at his house at Charing) between 16 and 18 July, and then returned to Norwich where he stayed until at least 6 October. A short trip to London (again not Charing) via Ipswich was followed by another long stay in Norwich for fully nine months between 17 October 1384 and 17 July 1385, when he left to join the royal army proceeding towards Scotland. Reappearing at Norwich on 30 August he remained there, except for a flying visit to London in January 1386, until 23 March 1387. He then went off to join the Earl of Arundel's sea expedition until about 15 April,[95] and then appears to have taken root in Norwich until 8 October.[96] Only then does he begin to move about again; but for a long time he prefers to be at Hoxne when he is not in his see city.

For an active man like Bishop Henry this behaviour was unusual. It is true that for part of the time his temporalities were forfeit, which prevented him from moving about in the usual way. The references to London, as distinct from Charing, suggest that his house there was barred to him and he had to find lodgings elsewhere. His temporalities were restored at the very end of 1385,[97] but for a long time afterwards his pattern of life, centred on Norwich, did not change.

A possible explanation could be that Henry Despenser was a manic depressive. In such people capacity for unusual energy, which he certainly displayed, can be contrasted with periods of profound depression. For example, from the end of 1383 to the autumn of 1387 he failed to attend any session of Parliament. On the other hand reliance on an episcopal register is not altogether safe, for it will not record events with which it is not directly concerned. But there is a clear pattern, and a few years later it occurs again.[98]

Several years elapsed before the effects of the crusade were finally dead and buried. In November 1387 various knights were appointed to inspect

77

proceedings in the constable and marshal's court regarding a prisoner by the name of John Sauce, who had been captured in Flanders during the Bishop of Norwich's expedition. Sauce was the prisoner in dispute in the case of Chamberlain versus Gerard in that court. Chamberlain called the marshal of Despenser's host, who testified that the ordinances he had made about the taking of prisoners made it impossible for Gerard to have taken the prisoner in question legitimately. M.H. Keen points out how carefully courts of this kind reviewed cases that came before them both in France and England. Friend and foe could expect to be treated with equal fairness according to the laws of war. Chivalry, after all, was an international concept.[99]

Over three years later the same court was much exercised by a plea in which Henry, Bishop of Norwich, was the plaintiff and William, Lord Hilton, the defendant. This also arose out of events in Flanders, where Hilton had led a retinue of men-at-arms and archers, a fact we would not have known about otherwise. Most annoyingly the nature of the charges against Hilton is not given, but they occupied the attention of an array of bishops, knights and legal experts. At first the decision went against Hilton, but he appealed, and later it was the Bishop who complained that justice had not been done to him. The proceedings dragged on from January 1391 until March 1394, when two extra knights and three clerks were added to the list of commissioners, 'the commissioners first named being too busy to attend thereto.'[100] Thus, on a note of total bathos, ends this account of Bishop Henry and the Flanders Crusade.

Notes

1. Sir Robert Carbonell, a close friend of Bishop Henry, died while on pilgrimage to the Holy Land.

2. Edouard Perroy, *L'Angleterre et la Schisme D'Occident,* Paris, dated 1933, p. 188, note 1. Besides the contemporary chronicles I have used Perroy extensively for this chapter, together with Norman Housley, *The Bishop of Norwich's Crusade, May 1383,* in *History Today*[33], May 1983, pp. 16-20. Professor Perroy was able to make use of A. P.R. Coulborn, *The Economic and Political Preliminaries of the Crusade of Henry Despenser, Bishop of Norwich, in 1383* (unpublished London Ph.D thesis, 1931). Recently C. Tyerman, *England and the Crusades 1095-1588,* has printed details of late medieval crusades against heathens, with a section on 'national' crusades, including that led by Henry Despenser.

3. Perroy, op. cit., p. 176.

4. Ibid, p. 178.

5. Ibid, p. 178.

6. Ibid, p. 171.

7. Ibid, pp. 174-175. M. McKisack, *The Fourteenth Century,* Oxford, 1959, p. 430.

8. Ibid, p. 182.

9. Ibid, pp. 184-185.

10. Ibid, p. 187. They could accompany the army only with the Bishop's express permission.

11. Ibid, p. 189, note 5. Philpot also helped to pay for the ships carrying the expedition. His generosity was most

welcome to the government on several occasions. (Walsingham, *Historia Anglicana*, ii, p. 96.) He, also, was in bad odour with John of Gaunt. (Antonia Gransden, *Historical Writing in England*, London, 1982, p. 139.)

12. Ibid, p. 190, note 3.

13. Ibid, p. 196, note 3.

14. Register, FF158V-159R. This entry is supported by the original acquittance.

15. Perroy, op. cit., p. 186.

16. St Mark, chapter 12, verses 41-44.

17. Walsingham, *Historia Anglicana*, ii, pp. 76-80. The form of absolution is on pp. 79-80. See also Perroy, op. cit., p. 187.

18. *Eulogium Historiarum*, ed. F.C. Haydon, Rolls Series, 1863, iii, p. 356. The first official indulgence for the dead was given by Pope Sixtus IV in 1476, almost a hundred years later. I owe this reference to Dr Diana Wood.

19. For his protest see H.B. Workman, *John Wyclif*, Oxford, 1926, ii, p. 67 and references there given.

20. Perroy, op. cit., p. 187: Workman, op. cit., ii, p. 67.

21. K.B. Macfarlane, *John Wyclif and the Beginnings of English Nonconformity*, English Universities Press, 1952, p. 126. For John Aston's preaching see *Henrici Knighton........monachi Leycestrensis*, ed. J. R. Lumby, Rolls Series, 1895, ii, p. 178. For Northwold and Corringham see A. K. McHardy, *Bishop Buckingham and the Lollards of Lincoln Diocese* in *Studies in Church History*[9], 1972, pp. 132-133 and 138.

22. Walsingham, op. cit., ii, p. 85.

23. Knighton, op. cit., ii, p. 198. Housley, op. cit., p. 18.

24. Housley, op. cit., p. 18.

25. Perroy, op. cit., p. 186, note 5.

26. *Calendar of Papal Letters, 1362-1396*, pp. 283-284.

27. Like Richard Ysmonger (*C.P.R.*, 1381-1385, p. 238) – by the Archbishop of Canterbury, no less.

28. *C.P.R.*, 1381-1385, p. 350.

29. *Eulogium Historiarum*, iii, p. 356.

30. *Victoria County History*, Norfolk, vol. 2, p. 339.

31. Walsingham, *Historia Anglicana*, ii, p. 90.

32. Ibid., pp. 85-86.

33. Housley, op. cit., p. 18.

34. Ibid., p. 19.

35. *C.CL.R.*, 1381-1385, pp. 256, 259, 261.

36. *C.CL.R.*, 1381-1385, pp. 259-260, 264.

37. *C.CL.R.*, 1381-1385, p. 261.

38. Ibid.

39. Register, F86V.

40. Register, F87R.

41. Register, F88R. Walsingham, *Historia Anglicana*, ii, p. 88.

42. Register, FF86V-89V. See below, p.95-96.

43. *C.CL.R.*, 1381-1385, pp. 260-261.

44. *C.P.R.*, 1381-1385, p. 265.

45. *C.CL.R.*, 1381-1385, p. 305.

46. J. J. N. Palmer, *England, France and Christendom 1377-1399*, London, 1972, page 49.

47. Perroy, op. cit., p. 190.

48. Walsingham, *Historia Anglicana,* ii, p. 94.

49. Walsingham, op. cit., ii, pp. 88-89. Housley, op. cit., p. 19. But in spite of the laws of war that applied this was ostensibly a crusade, and the prerogative of mercy might, perhaps, have been exercised. This highlights the ambiguous nature of the whole crusade. See also *Polychronicon Ranulphi,* Higden, ed. J. R. Lumby, Rolls Series, 1882, vol. 8, p. 464. W. A. Pantin, 'A Medieval Treatise on Letter-writing With Examples', in *Bulletin of the John Rylands Library,* XIII, 1929, p. 360.

50. Walsingham, *Historia Anglicana,* ii, p. 91.

51. Ibid., p. 92.

52. Ibid. Higden's *Continuator* says almost 11,000 with only 15 killed on the English side. (Vol. 8, p. 465.) The *Westminster Chronicler* says 10,000, and that a Te Deum was sung in thanksgiving. (ibid, 9, pp. 18-19.) The letter printed by Pantin also gives 10,000 'at least'.

53. Walsingham, *Historia Anglicana,* ii, pp. 94-95. Housley, op. cit., p. 19.

54. Pantin, op. cit., pp. 359-364.

55. Margaret Aston, 'The Impeachment of Bishop Despenser', in *Bulletin of the Institute of Historical Research,* vol. XXXVIII, no. 98, November, 1965, pp. 127-148. See also Higden, op. cit., 9, pp. 18-19.

56. Housley, op. cit., p. 19.

57. Walsingham, *Historia Anglicana,* ii, pp. 95.

58. Housley, op. cit., pp. 19-20.

59. Walsingham, *Historia Anglicana,* ii, p. 96.

60. Ibid.

61. Ibid, p. 98.

62. Housley, op. cit., p. 20.

63. Ibid.

64. Walsingham, *Historia Anglica,* ii, pp. 98-99. Knighton (op. cit., p. 199) says that there was only one large gun called the gun of Canterbury, together with a trepget (trebuchet or catapult) and a *'machinam magnam',* whatever that was. A siege could not properly begin until guns or other siege engines had been discharged by the besiegers. (M.H. Keen, *The Laws of War in the Late Middle Ages,* London and Toronto, 1965, pp. 119ff.) The breaking of the siege was afterwards commemorated in Ypres by the festival of Thuyndag. Celebrated on the first Sunday in August it kept in mind the way in which a barricade of garden trellises had been erected on the wall to strengthen it against the besiegers. (David Nicholas, *Medieval Flanders,* New York, 1992, p. 358.

65. Perroy, op. cit., p. 195. According to the *Westminster Chronicle* Bishop Henry proposed a night attack on the advance guard of the French army before it came too close. (Higden, op. cit., 9, pp. 21-22.)

66. Walsingham, *Historia Anglicana,* ii, p. 104.

67. Ibid, pp. 99-100.

68. Ibid, p. 101. Higden, op. cit., 8, p. 465.

69. Ibid, p. 101. Perroy, op. cit., p. 199. The Westminster chronicler in Higden, op. cit., 9, p. 22 estimates that the captains received 28,000 francs in all.

70. Ibid, pp. 102-103.

71. Perroy, op. cit., p. 199.

72. *C.CL.R.,* 1381-1385, pp. 368-369. In spite of this Foulmere retained or regained the Bishop's trust, as he appointed him Archdeacon of Suffolk on 4th July, 1387. (Register, F122V.)

73. Anne's father was of course the Emperor Charles IV. They may also have seen the Despenser altarpiece if it

had been completed at the time of their visit.

74. Walsingham, *Historia Anglicana*, ii, pp. 102-103, quoting from Horace, *De Arte Poetica*, i, p. 139.

75. Aston, op. cit., pp. 144-145.

76. McKisack, op. cit., p. 432, note 1.

77. Perroy, op. cit., p. 200, note 4, quoting *Letter Book H of the City of London*, London, 1907, p. 218.

78. Register, F96V.

79. The main, and very detailed, source for the proceedings against Bishop Henry is Margaret Aston, 'The Impeachment of Bishop Despenser' (see note 55 above), which will be cited from now on as Impeachment.

80. Impeachment, p. 146.

81. Froissart says he had only 600 lances and 1,500 others (quoted by Workman, op. cit., ii, p. 69).

82. Impeachment, p. 131. The reference to 6,000 or 7,000 men suggests that the army had reached its proper strength and more. We do not know, however, how many of these were men-at-arms or archers or, indeed, enthusiasts of little or no military value. When these men had returned to England their circumstances could still be desperate. Colin Paine points to evidence that in 1384 Battle Abbey was still giving relief to destitute returned crusaders.

83. Impeachment, p. 131.

84. Ibid.

85. *Eulogium Historiarum*, ut supra, iii, p. 356. The writer's judgement of the Bishop is that he was 'magis militari levitate dissolutus quam pontificali maturitate solidus' (more of a foolish and dissolute soldier than a mature and responsible prelate).

86. McKisack, op. cit., p. 433, note 2.

87. See above, pp. 9-10.

88. Impeachment, p. 131.

89. *C.P.R.*, 1381-1385, pp. 414, 476. *C.CL.R.*, 1381-1385, p. 368.

90. *C.CL.R.*, 1381-1385, p. 368. Fitz Rauf's crimes are also mentioned in *C.P.R.*, 1381-1385, p. 405.

91. Walsingham, *Historia Anglicana*, ii, p. 104.

92. Ibid, p. 156.

93. Ibid, p. 77.

94. *C.CL.R.*, 1381-1385, p. 457.

95. See p.118 below.

96. Register, FF96V-125V.

97. Register, F113V. On 31st December, 1385, he bestows the deanery of Dunwich 'in pleno iure' (in full right).

98. For a medical description of manic depression see The I.C.D. 10 Classification of Mental and Behavioural Disorders, The World Health Organisation, Geneva, 1992, pp. 113ff. Hypomania, a lesser degree of mania, can be marked by conceit and boorish behaviour. From these, particularly in his earlier years, Henry Despenser was not exempt.

99. *C.P.R.*, 1385-1389, pp. 394-395.

100. *C.P.R.*, 1391-1396, pp. 17, 306, 390.

5. The Controversial Bishop

Those who take a poor view of Henry Despenser point out, among other things, that he was much given to controversy. Men of God are supposed, wherever possible, to promote peace among others and seek after it themselves. In this, to put it mildly, he was not very successful.

On the other hand all religious superiors were held to be responsible for the possessions of their church, monastery or cathedral to the saint or saints to whom it was dedicated. In the case of Norwich this was the Holy Trinity, an awesome responsibility for which answer would have to be made at the Last Judgement. This may well explain why some apparently petty jurisdictional disputes were pursued with much vigour over a long period of time.

Very much in this tradition Henry had a long-running feud with the prior and monks who served his own cathedral church. He also became embroiled with St Albans Abbey, then the most prestigious monastery in England and the one that, through Thomas Walsingham and his school of history, was best able to publicise its point of view and lambast its opponents. Not content with that, he tangled with a local offshoot of the international monastic order of Cluny. When it came to secular authorities he seems to have been implicated in a controversy that led to murder. But most notorious of all was his clash with the people of Lynn in 1377, which left him with considerably more than his pride damaged. Lynn, in fact, is a good place at which to start this investigation.

But before doing so, one or two general points may usefully be made. First Henry was a civil lawyer by training and also, it seems, by inclination. He appears to have enjoyed the challenge of taking on other centres of power and authority, be they personal or corporate. Not for him the modern wisdom that one goes to law only as a very last resort.

Many others beside Henry found it desirable, if not imperative, to study law. The Church, of course, had a complex and extensive legal system of its own, and skilled practitioners like John Darlington, his Official Principal and right hand man in the diocese for so many years, were always needed to find their way through its thickets. But insofar as the Church was always enmeshed with the world through its possession of lands, rights and privileges, all very much in the secular arena, it needed civil lawyers too.

Bishop Henry Despenser was a litigious person. But the age in which he lived was a highly litigious age. Unless you were at the very bottom of the social complex you would have possessions, rights and privileges, even if they were quite modest. And the very fact of having them demanded that you should be able, in person or through an advocate, to defend them if someone else tried to take them away. As the age in question could also be a violent age you might even have to resort to other means if proper legal safeguards were wanting. The legal game was one that many medieval people seem to have enjoyed playing. Its rules were simple. At all costs hold on to what you have; but if a chance comes to gain possession of someone else's rights and possessions, then take it.

Henry Despenser played that game enthusiastically. As soon as he became bishop he identified himself with the maintenance, and if possible the extension, of the episcopal rights and privileges he had inherited. Indeed this was an attitude that, at least so far as maintenance was concerned, was expected of him as of all diocesan bishops. If this required him to take up a particular standpoint, he did so. But he was far from being alone in this. Instances are known where a man, changing his work, adopted the positions and attitudes associated with his new responsibility, even if these were quite contrary to those he had espoused in the past. The classic example of this is Thomas Becket, Archbishop of Canterbury, who changed from being an exemplary servant to a thorn in Henry II's flesh - and eventually a martyr - when he took on a spiritual role that would naturally cause him to oppose his master's outlook and policy fundamentally. In fact he warned Henry that this would happen were he to become archbishop.

But an example much closer to Bishop Henry is also available. Soon after he became Prior of the cathedral monastery of the Holy Trinity, in 1382, Alexander Totington found himself in opposition to his episcopal superior. But when, in 1406, he was elected bishop himself he changed right round and adopted all the claims and contentions he had only recently strenuously opposed. And no one seems to have thought it surprising.

A corollary to all this, that may bear investigation, is the question of the personal relationship between those who found themselves, because of the positions they held, on opposite sides of a legal argument. In our own day litigants are not usually the best of friends except, perhaps, in the occasional collusive action where the purpose, entirely amicable, is to find out exactly what the law says. But I suspect that this was not always the case in medieval times, when official and personal attitudes might not necessarily coincide.

Turning to Bishop Henry's controversy with Lynn, his register reveals that he was there on 7 June 1377, so it was on that day, or one very close to it, that his celebrated confrontation with the townsfolk took place.[1] For all its bias against the Bishop the account in Thomas Walsingham's *Chronicon Angliæ* is probably reasonably accurate.[2]

It would appear that the visit was formal, for on his arrival in the town Henry was met by the civic dignitaries, headed by the Mayor, before whom a mace was being carried. When bishops of Norwich had previously visited the town a wand had been carried before them, but he was not prepared to accept this. He insisted on being preceded by the mace because he saw himself as possessing the final authority over the town and all who lived in it. To this the aldermen replied that they would be happy to comply if, but only if, the Bishop gained acceptance for this new custom from the King and his council; otherwise they feared that the lower orders, who were given to riotous behaviour, would react in an unseemly fashion. Clearly they were afraid of being stoned, to the extent that they begged him on bended knee to desist for his own honour as well as theirs because of the danger they would be in if he refused to moderate his attitude. But to no avail: like Rehoboam of old[3] – another young man – Henry rejected this wise advice and persisted in his rash demands, calling the elders of the town cowards and the common people ribalds, an emphatic contemporary term of abuse.

In a final effort to ward off disaster, the aldermen respectfully asked him to excuse them from conducting him out of the town, for they were afraid that the mob might even kill them if it got the impression that they were siding with the Bishop. Yet again Henry refused to listen, and instead ordered one of the aldermen to carry the mace before him. After the procession had gone a little way all hell was let loose. The town gates were shut, and the Bishop and his party were assailed with stones, arrows and other weapons. He himself was wounded, his horse bolted, and as darkness fell his retinue left him alone and fled. Fortunately he was able to take refuge in the priory of St Margaret, or his episcopal career might have ended there and then.[4]

The consequences of this violence were, of course, far-reaching. On 16 June the outraged Bishop secured from the King the appointment of a commission of oyer and terminer (hear and determine) to look into the whole affair. This recites his complaint that twenty-three named townspeople, with others, assaulted him at Bishop's Lynn, followed him to the priory of St Margaret with the intention of killing him, besieged him there so that he could not freely minister to the people, killed twenty of his horses and assaulted his men and servants.[5]Two days later he unleashed an even more potent spiritual weapon when he persuaded Archbishop Simon Sudbury to lay an interdict on the town, thus depriving it for the time being of all the rites and sacraments of the Church.[6]

Then, on 12 July, word came from the new King's council that on pain of ferocious penalties (a fine of £2,000 and forfeiture of possessions) the contending parties should do no further harm to each other.[7]With such a threat hanging over them the matter was finally settled with the aid of arbitration from the sheriffs of Norfolk and Cambridge: but by then the town was worse off by no less than £515 5s. 5d.[8]This may or may not have included the sum of £100 the mayor and community granted to William Holmetone and Thomas Sparram in consideration of the injuries they received during the dispute with the servants of Bishop Henry Despenser.[9] Clearly the fighting was not all one-sided.

To judge from the royal letter mentioned above, both parties were felt to share the blame equally. Dean Goulburn, however, was of the opinion that the Bishop was within his rights, and 'the gentry of the diocese and the council inclined to support him rather than the townspeople'.[10] This is true enough, but does not address the main question, which is whether rights should be enforced even when prudence dictates otherwise.

It is appropriate to examine the facts of this unseemly quarrel. In the first place Bishop Henry, by his intervention, had not ruptured a situation where perfect peace existed before. Far from it. A dispute between town and bishop had been going on since the opening years of the thirteenth century. On 14 September 1204, King John had granted the men of Lynn a free borough and a gild merchant, but reserving the existing rights of the Bishop of Norwich and the Earl of Arundel.[11] This had been followed, on 24 March 1205, by a charter from the bishop of the time granting the townsmen all the liberties enjoyed by the town of Oxford, saving the liberties and customs he already held.[12]

This, of course, meant that unlike Great Yarmouth, which was given a royal charter at much the same time, the men of Lynn were not entirely free to order their own affairs. Such a situation naturally rankled; there was more trouble in 1234 and further echoes of the continuing dispute may be discerned in 1309, when John Salmon was bishop,[13] and even more in 1352. In that year Bishop William Bateman concluded a composition with the mayor, burgesses and community of Lynn. The latter agreed not to press for the rights vested in the Bishop, which the king had granted to him. But they were allowed to choose their mayor, on condition that the man chosen presented himself within three days at the Bishop's manor at Gaywood. There he was to swear an oath to the Bishop himself if he happened to be present, or to his steward or to some other official of the liberty if he was not.[14] This state of affairs still prevailed when Henry Despenser became bishop in 1370.

The ill-fated visit of 1377 was not his first. He undoubtedly visited the town in 1373 before issuing his constitutions, already mentioned, regarding the conduct of its clergy.[15] He also carried out a visitation in 1376 which seems to have passed off peacefully, though Workman attributes this to the liberal provision of wine for his refreshment, which cost the town £1 6s. 10.[16] Even so, with his legal acumen, Bishop Henry should have known that because of the long-standing dispute unexpected problems might arise which would need to be handled carefully. This he conspicuously failed to do. But one question has

Bishop Henry Despenser – misericord in St Margaret's, King's Lynn

never been asked or answered. Why did he go to Lynn in the first place? It was certainly not to indulge in amiable sociability.

A possible clue is to be found in his register. Just four days earlier, on 3 June 1377, he is recorded as being at Great Yarmouth.[17] Now this is unusual: he very rarely went to Yarmouth and for two reasons. In the first place the borough, unlike Lynn, was completely independent. He had no rights there. Secondly, the church in the town was entirely under the control of the prior and convent of Norwich. The great church of St Nicholas combined monastic and parochial functions. At the east end the small group of monks recited their offices, and at the west end chaplains appointed by the priory ministered to the people of the town. Unless some really serious disciplinary matter arose the Bishop had little reason to interfere.

It followed that when he did venture in that direction he tended to go as a soldier rather than as an ecclesiastic. On 3 June 1377, King Edward III, long in physical and moral decline, had only eighteen days to live. His son, the re-nowned Edward the Black Prince, had predeceased him, leaving a young son and the prospect of a prolonged minority. Well aware of this, the French saw a golden opportunity to make mischief and take revenge. Raids on the south coast were intensified; invasion could not be ruled out. England was swept by a wave of apprehension and fear; so it is possible that Bishop Henry's visit to Yarmouth was connected with its defences rather than with its spiritual health. The further possibility that no one had asked him to make such a visit is quite beside the point. He never had any problem about acting on his own initiative.

So when he moved straight on to Lynn, as the register indicates, it seems at least possible that he went with the same errand. Lynn, of course, was not in such a vulnerable position as Yarmouth, but neither was it entirely safe. It was also, in a very real sense, his responsibility. Its well-known riches could still fall to a determined assault. But if this was Bishop Henry's purpose in going there –

The Black Prince – misericord in St Margaret's, King's Lynn

to advise on defensive measures – that purpose was never fulfilled. Instead, he allowed himself to be embroiled in a foolish dispute about rights and precedence with disastrous results. In doing so, as E.F. Jacob points out, he revealed his ignorance of the fact that Lynn itself was beset by faction. Municipal life was marred by continual squabbles between the leading men or *potentiores*, the middling people, the *mediocres*, and the lower orders, proletariat or mob, the *inferiores*. By acting as he did he added fuel to the flames. He would have done much better to heed the warnings of the aldermen, who knew only too well what the situation was. And in any case someone like Bishop Henry should have known that strife of this kind frequently occurred in London and in other cities and towns elsewhere in England.[18]

So one can have a little sympathy with the verdict of the St Albans chronicler, probably Thomas Walsingham himself, when he refers to Bishop Henry as '*iuvenis et effrenis*' – young and unrestrained.[19] In medieval times to be 34, which was his age in 1377, was to be no longer young, but his actions were certainly those of a young man, and his physical appearance may possibly have enhanced such an impression. Of course we have no way of knowing; but the misericord beneath the prior's stall in the church of St Margaret, King's Lynn shows Bishop Henry, identified by the Despenser arms, as a decidedly youthful prelate with rounded features. By contrast the next stall shows Edward the Black Prince as a man ravaged by illness.[20] Perhaps the prince was recently dead when these faces were carved, suggesting a very early attempt at portraiture and a date ranging from the late 1370s to the early 1380s. This is confirmed by a surviving account roll of the priory, for the period 1379-1380, where it is stated that the stalls are not yet finished *(nondum finitur)*.[21] The stalls themselves are reminiscent of the set at Lincoln Cathedral, completed not long before.

After the major unpleasantness in 1377, both sides seem to have drawn back from further confrontation. Indeed, relations seem to have been amicable for the remainder of the century. In 1383, with the agreement of the prior and convent of Norwich, the Bishop gave the Austin Friars of Lynn a small piece of land at Gaywood, from which a spring issued, to provide them with a water supply.[22] Nine years later he granted the Mayor and burgesses the privilege of building a water mill or mills in the 'Flete' at Lynn for a rent of twenty shillings a year.[23]

Moreover, only two years after he had been so roughly handled he became involved, quite acceptably it seems, in an internal dispute which gave Lynn a great deal of trouble. The people who attended St Nicholas, a daughter church of the priory of St Margaret, continually pressed to have all the sacraments of the church, including holy baptism, freely available there. A papal privilege agreeing to this had been issued, and a chaplain, John Peye, was seeking to have it renewed.[24] This of course was contrary to the interests of St Margaret's, not to mention the prior and convent of Norwich, who had final authority over it. Those who objected to the pressure from St Nicholas were backed up by the leaders of the community, for the Mayor and thirty burgesses conducted a test by walking the distance between the two churches. They then decided that the St Nicholas people would suffer no hardship by being required to attend St Margaret's to receive the sacraments in question. Papal judges delegate also reported in favour of St Margaret's, and Bishop Henry was required to terminate the matter. This he did by sub-delegating Walter, prior of the Augustinian priory of Pentney, who after careful enquiry gave a final decision in favour of St Margaret's on 1 March, 1382.[25] However, by 1432, well after Bishop Henry's time, the Mayor and community of Lynn had changed their minds completely, and were petitioning the prior and convent of Norwich in support of renewed pressure to allow a font to be installed at St Nicholas.[26]

But with the accession of Henry IV further trouble arose. The Bishop was accused, among other things prejudicial to the town, of failing to repair a staithe or quay there called Le Bysshopstathe, thus endangering the town's defences against flooding.[27] This dispute rumbled on for a considerable time and was made worse by the mutual dislike of King and Bishop. Without going into burdensome detail Bishop Henry, while maintaining all due courtesy, was clearly determined not to attend the court of a man he regarded as a usurper, even when pressure was put upon him to do so. As we have seen, even his gallstones were pressed into service as a convenient excuse.[28] On his side, King Henry, also outwardly polite, was quite openly prejudiced in favour of the town, which is now referred to as 'the king's town and borough of Lenne'.[29] For his part the Bishop clearly felt under pressure, as a letter of his that has been preserved reveals. Writing to an unnamed Justice of the Peace between 1401 and 1404 he begs him to be at Lynn on St James's Day, when legal proceedings against Henry are to be held. Several of the jury empanelled for the purpose dare not appear because of the threats made by townsmen against them, and members of his own episcopal council have also been warned off.[30] Others may simply have been unwilling to get involved. For example, on 2 November 1403, Sir William Calthorpe was let off twenty pounds from the revenues forfeited by him for not taking his place on the jury in a dispute between the King and the Bishop.[31] Even the Bishop's death did not prevent this dispute from dragging on until the sixteenth century.

One might conclude from all this that Bishop Henry's relationship with Lynn left much to be desired. In mitigation it may be said, as was not always realised by his detractors, that the dispute was not of his making and that dissension within the town itself tended to make things worse than they would have been otherwise.

Without doubt Lynn was a rich and important place. It sheltered merchants of international repute, like the men commemorated by the great Braunche and Walsoken brasses in St Margaret's church, men to whose feasts the King himself would be glad to go.[32] But we must now turn our attention to St Albans. Situated only a few miles to the north of London, and on one of the most important roads in the kingdom, its famous abbey was ideally placed for gathering information. Travellers of all descriptions passed by, and many turned aside to accept hospitality from the monastic house which, for some time now, had replaced Glastonbury as the most prestigious in the kingdom. In the previous century, in the days of Matthew Paris, it had become an unrivalled school of historical writing; and as the fourteenth century approached its end the same tradition had been rekindled under Thomas Walsingham and an outstanding abbot, Thomas de la Mare.

But in 1394 Walsingham's secure vantage point in the centre of affairs was rudely upset. He was sent to be Prior of Wymondham, the most important of the abbey's many daughter houses.[33] In all probability it was a move dictated by monastic obedience rather than any sort of ambition; the more senior monks could expect occasional 'postings' of this kind. But although Wymondham was a town of reasonable size, and the high road to Norwich passed by, it was still very much a backwater compared with St Albans. So it is not surprising that Walsingham did not remain prior of Wymondham for long.[34]

The Wymondham posting may have been unwelcome for another reason. When Walsingham presented himself at South Elmham to take his oath of obedience – carefully qualified as we have seen[35] – he found himself in the formidable presence of a man about whom a chronicle prepared by him, or under

89

his supervision, speaks in a most unflattering way. He might well have had uncomfortable memories of the violent dispute between his abbey and this bishop that had occurred fourteen years previously and had occasioned those rude comments.

What had happened? Whenever the clergy granted the king, by way of taxation, a tenth of their annual income, or a subsidy (a graded tax based on different ecclesiastical ranks), a mandate would go to the bishops requiring them to collect it within their dioceses in person or by deputy. Needless to say, they never took personal responsibility but delegated the highly unwelcome, unpopular and time-consuming task to some priest or priests with sufficient position and authority to do it effectively. But on 10 May 1380, the officials of the royal exchequer sent an indignant letter to the Bishop of Norwich.[36] They complained that although his diocese contained many suitable clergy of sufficient seniority to act as his deputy for collecting the subsidy recently granted he had passed them all over and had appointed the Prior of Wymondham as collector for the archdeaconries of Norwich and Norfolk. But the Prior of Wymondham, as they pointed out, could not be charged with any such responsibility, as his priory was exempt from the Bishop's jurisdiction and, like the mother house at St Albans, was answerable only to the Pope. In view of the Bishop's action the Prior had been recalled to St Albans by his Abbot, where soon afterwards he was made archdeacon. What is more, the subsidy remained uncollected in Norfolk 'at which the King is very greatly astonished and moved as he well may be.' Having, one suspects, put these words into the royal mouth the Exchequer officials demanded that Bishop Henry should appoint someone else to be his delegate, tell the government who it was, and see to it that the subsidy be collected by the feast of St John the Baptist (24 June), in other words, in a month and a half's time at the latest. Otherwise, if through his default the subsidy remained unpaid after the said term, 'the King will betake himself heavily against him'.

But the deadline came and went without any payment, so on the following day (25 June), the King and council wrote to Bishop Henry again.[37] They had heard the Abbot's contention that Wymondham was completely outside any episcopal jurisdiction, and that in any case the Prior was the Abbot's nominee removable at will. But they were also aware that the Bishop might have had a case too, and that what had been put to them on behalf of St Albans was not necessarily the whole truth. Clearly, they went on, such a complex matter could not be resolved quickly, but meanwhile they needed the subsidy money and requested the Bishop to nominate suitable and discreet men to collect it. But the Bishop had replied with excuses that on examination proved to be wanton and insufficient. For his part, the King had no intention of foregoing any longer the money the government so badly needed because of a dispute that had nothing to do with him, so Henry received a peremptory command to have the subsidy collected and paid in to the Exchequer by 20 July, the feast of St Margaret the Virgin, 'so demeaning himself in this matter that the arduous affairs of the King and realm remain not undone through his defaults whereby the King would have cause to proceed heavily against him as a contemner of the royal commands'.

It would seem, however, that not even this brought in the money that was owed. A full-scale legal action now began between bishop and abbey, and according to the chronicle, obviously a hostile witness, Bishop Henry tried more than once to recover the money owing in subsidy by getting it distrained from the goods of the priory. But in spite of bribery on his part – so it was alleged – the abbey's lawyers first persuaded the sheriff to take no action on the distraint, and then went to the royal council where they obtained a decision in their favour. In future the Prior of Wymondham was not to be molested in any way.[38]

Under the circumstances it is not surprising that the abbey chronicler really lets himself go in heaping abuse on Bishop Despenser. 'A man distinguished neither in learning nor discretion' he splutters; 'a youth unbridled and insolent'; 'as a bishop unstable' and 'like another Herod incapable of restraint' *(velut alter Herodes insaniens).*[39] The facts that Henry was nearer forty than thirty and had spent several years at Oxford were conveniently forgotten.

Many years later, on 10 July, 1399, Bishop Henry visited St Albans. A loyal partisan of Richard II, he was there with reinforcements for the army of the Duke of York, who was gathering what power he could to resist Henry Bolingbroke, soon to be Henry IV, as he marched south from Ravenspur. Under the circumstances the monks may have preferred to steer clear of possible involvement through offering hospitality. But it would be good to know if by then the breach had been healed.[40]

Did Bishop Henry learn anything from this reverse? At first sight it would appear that he did not. For when another subsidy became due from the diocese he nominated the Prior of Thetford to be his deputy for the collection.[41] From its foundation Thetford had belonged to the family of monasteries centred on the great abbey of Cluny in Burgundy. Thus, even more than Wymondham, it was outside the jurisdiction of the diocesan bishop. Entirely independent, the Cluniacs answered only to the Pope. Having seen what had happened at Wymondham the Prior of Thetford immediately applied to the King for help, and the latter, with his council, sent the Bishop of Norwich yet another stiff letter, telling him to cease molesting the Prior and appoint other fit persons to carry out the collection.

But in this instance Bishop Henry may have had a case worthy of being argued. As the Hundred Years War progressed monasteries dependent on a mother house in France became increasingly unpopular. The French monks were seen as potential if not actual spies, and the whole situation was fraught with difficulties. These were increased after 1378 by the Great Schism, during which France and England supported different popes, and mother house and daughter house would profess different allegiances. As time went on, a number of these houses, including several from the Cluniac order, applied for charters of denization, a corporate form of naturalisation. In this way their links with continental mother houses were finally broken, and they received the right to conduct their own affairs and elect their own superiors like any other English monastery. In the case of Thetford this occurred in 1376;[42] but the corollary to this development, which the monks there may not have noticed, was that it put them under the control of the local bishop. Henry, one assumes, did notice, hence his appointment of the Prior of Thetford as a tax collector. Nevertheless his strategy did not succeed, presumably because their former Cluniac associations, though now past history, could still be used by the monks to win their house exemption from such unwelcome chores.

How does one assess this behaviour on the part of Bishop Henry? It may well be that in some respects his personality was thoroughly difficult and cross-grained. But it is also likely that he enjoyed legal battles as much as the kind he was already used to as a soldier. Did he in fact relish the intellectual pleasure in probing the weak places of his opponent's defences? It seems that he had plausible cases in his confrontations with both St Albans and Thetford. Certainly the strength of the opposition did not worry him, especially during the earlier years of his episcopate. He cannot be accused of oppressing those weaker than he.

But did he have any other reason for acting in the way he did? Capgrave, as we have seen, applauds him as a conscientious and caring pastor. It is also clear that, like many other people of the day, he had little respect for those in high authority. This may have proceeded in part from his self-confidence and willingness to act on his own initiative, but the lack of respect was surely there. In the circumstances he might well have added his voice to the chorus of complaint against the constant and heavy taxation laid on the clergy during this period, suspecting that the proceeds would be misused rather than used.

Even so, what could he do about it? He could ease the burden on his clergy and keep the authorities at bay by deliberately suggesting methods of collection that would be unacceptable. This would bring about a delay as welcome to the ordinary clergy as it was distasteful to the clerks of the Exchequer with their perennial shortage of money. His adversaries of St Albans put out the alternative theory that by appointing the Prior of Wymondham to collect the subsidy he was really hoping for a substantial payment in cash as an inducement to overlook his refusal. Acceptance, of course, would have been tantamount to conceding all the Bishop's claims over the priory.

This is of course all conjecture. But it is interesting that the Bishop of St Davids was also an offender in this matter. He, too, had incurred the government's displeasure by failing to collect or forward two subsidies in succession. Indeed, it was felt that his offence was even greater than that of Bishop Henry, for as a former member of that government he should have appreciated the problems facing the State and given his full co-operation. Why did he not? One wonders whether he, in line with the theory suggested above, had also put the needs of his own clergy before those of a government far away whose bark, one suspects, was considerably worse than its bite.[43]

But the monks of St Albans, Wymondham and Thetford were not the only ones with whom the Bishop of Norwich contended. Other monks – those of his cathedral priory of the Holy Trinity – had an even closer relationship with their father-in-God. It is now time to look at his dealings with them. The seeds of trouble had been sown long before. In Norman times several English cathedral churches – Canterbury, Winchester, Worcester, Ely, Durham, Rochester, Chester and Norwich – had become, or remained, Benedictine monasteries. Another, Carlisle, was a convent of Augustinian canons. In all these cases the idea envisaged was that the bishop, besides being father-in-God to his diocese, should occupy the same position in relation to his cathedral as if he were its abbot. It was realised that the relationship, for obvious reasons, could not be as close as in an ordinary monastery, so a prior, himself a considerable personage, acted as its working head. To minds steeped in the theory and practice of monasticism this was an ideal arrangement, but it depended, of course, on the appointment of a succession of monk-bishops who would be in full sympathy with their brothers in the cloister. If, on the other hand, a bishop came from the ranks of the secular clergy, trouble could easily break out even with the best intentions on both sides, and often did. This perverse legacy was duly inherited by Bishop Henry Despenser and the monks of Holy Trinity, led by their Prior Nicholas of Hoo. The legacy was rendered still more perverse by the fact that as the bishops gave less attention to their monks, or quarrelled with them, so the prior gained in stature until he became a very important person indeed. As with other leading monasteries of a more conventional kind, heads of cathedral priories were often given, by the Pope, the coveted privilege of pontificalia – the mitre, staff, ring and gloves which were otherwise the prerogative of those in episcopal orders. Norwich itself, however, did not receive this privilege until 1519, in the time of Prior Robert Catton.[44]

It is clear that Henry Despenser's episcopate coincided with what Dom David Knowles called the most distinguished phase of the priory's history, which he placed between 1350 and 1420.[45] During that time it produced a group of theologians and administrators of high calibre. It made full use of Gloucester College, the Benedictine house of studies at Oxford, and its own library was well stocked. One of its monks, Adam Easton, became a cardinal at the Roman Curia, and another, Thomas Brunton or Brinton, was promoted to the bishopric of Rochester, where he soon acquired a reputation as the foremost preacher of the day. Both products of tiny villages in the Norwich hinterland, it is interesting to know that in the fourteenth century the talents of such men could be recognised and developed right up to such exalted levels.

Another talented local man was Prior Nicholas of Hoo, who had been in office since 1356.[46] He probably came from Sutton Hoo, near Woodbridge in Suffolk. Convention required that when a man took his monastic vows he shed his surname and was known from then on by the name of the place from which he came. Prior Catton, who has just been mentioned, is a case in point: Catton (nowadays Old Catton) is a place just outside Norwich. As there were so many monasteries it followed that most recruited from an area reasonably close at hand, though a monastery that was also a cathedral might attract candidates from further afield, at least from within the diocesan boundaries.

Nicholas of Hoo was appointed one of Bishop Henry's deputies as soon as the latter became bishop.[47] Not unnaturally he was less occupied than his fellow Vicar-General Master Roger Yonge of Sutton, but by a happy arrangement he often admitted to office priors of smaller monasteries in the diocese, who would appreciate the ministry of a fellow monk.

After twenty-five years as cathedral prior Nicholas was succeeded by a man of impeccable local origin, Alexander Totington, who came from a village not far from Aylsham. On 14 April 1382, Bishop Henry admitted him to office in the chapel of his manor of Thorpe St Andrew, and he was installed 'as is the custom' in the cathedral church by John Darlington, Official Principal.[48] Totington, like his predecessor, was to serve for a quarter of a century as prior, but he was destined for still greater things after that.

As prior he soon renewed acquaintance with John Darlington. Just over a year after Alexander's appointment Bishop Henry, about to leave for Flanders and the crusade, made careful dispositions for the running of the diocese while he was away. Among these was a commission to Darlington, Master John Clemens and Master Stephen Holt, giving them power to remove and absolve officials of the cathedral church of Norwich.[49] The next month John Darlington exercised these powers by presiding in the chapter-house when Brother John Marsham was appointed subprior, or second-in-command, in the place of

Brother William Thetford.[50]

So far as one can see there was no immediate trouble. John Darlington could be trusted to do his part sensibly and tactfully. And although there may have been strong feelings that the Bishop, through his commission, was exceeding his powers, it was hardly a propitious moment to say so when the prelate in question was levying war against schismatics, especially French ones.

But such feelings would not have lasted for long. After the failure of the crusade Bishop Henry returned to his diocese a very diminished man. There was no longer any reason why the Prior and his monks should not press their point of view in the matters that lay between them and their bishop. Indeed, given Henry's temper of mind, he may well have relieved his disappointment by resorting to legal war in place of its military equivalent.

E.H. Carter says that the dispute began in earnest in 1386.[51] It continued until the Bishop's death in 1406 and even beyond that, so that a settlement of the complex issues involved was not achieved until 1411, through the arbitration of Archbishop Thomas Arundel. Both E.H. Carter and Norman Tanner[52] devote space to the quarrel.

First of all, what was the dispute all about? Tanner suggests[53] that Bishop Henry was at odds with the Prior and monks over the internal administration of their monastery and the part he ought to play in it. Crucial issues were the admission of novices, the profession and punishment of monks, appointment to, and removal from, the many executive offices required for the smooth running of the priory and other matters to do with the management of its property, the Bishop's right of visitation, and the payment of various tithes and dues he himself owed to the monks. Another issue, which came to the fore after Bishop Henry's time, was that of the reverencialia, or formal acts of respect and welcome, that the monks owed to their father-in-God when he visited his cathedral in an official capacity. For this, like the trouble at Lynn, was a long-running affair in which several others participated beside Bishop Henry Despenser and Prior Alexander Totington.

Secondly, who was involved beside the Bishop and the monks? The dispute caused much concern and heart-searching, even at the highest levels of church and state. Three successive archbishops of Canterbury were drawn in; William Courtenay until his death in 1396, Thomas Arundel his successor, both before and after his temporary deposition and exile by order of Richard II, and Roger Walden, who briefly supplanted him. All seem to have done their best to bring about an agreement. Courtenay died when his arbitration was showing promise of success, and the dispute began all over again.[54] Other diocesan bishops also became involved. Then, of course, there was the Pope and the various legal experts at Rome who were delegated to try and find a solution. Finally there was

95

Richard II himself, whose efforts were compromised in the eyes of the prior and monks by his warm and long-standing friendship with their bishop. With these three centres of power and responsibility involved, any-one who disliked an opinion or a suggested solution offered by one of them could easily appeal against it to another, thus confusing the situation. By emphasising the power of the church they could bypass the King, and if they preferred the latter's standpoint they could take a patriotic line and deplore legal cases originating in England being sent out of the country.

By the opening years of the fifteenth century the Prior and convent, still dissatisfied by Archbishop Arundel's latest effort at conciliation, were apparently so thoroughly weary of the whole business that they agreed to pay Bishop Henry 400 marks in order to keep their privileges. In this connection Carter quotes an ancient writer, Alexander Nevill, whose outspoken condemnation of the Bishop has certainly contributed to the bad reputation he suffers today.[55]

But even that was not the end of the matter. Shortly afterwards Bishop Despenser died; his erstwhile opponent Alexander Totington succeeded him, and at once changed sides, as has been mentioned already. So the dispute began all over again.[56] Eventually Archbishop Arundel came to Norwich on a formal visitation, and with his advisers hammered out a decree which concluded the matter. This, printed in full by Carter, examines the disputed questions in detail, and while apparently favouring the Bishop effectively comes down on the side of the Prior and convent.[57] Even so, the controversy had to wait until the time of Bishop Lyhart (1446-1472) before being finally laid to rest, and the question of reverencialia was still in dispute when Bishop Goldwell visited the cathedral priory in 1492.[58]

Those considering this lamentable story might think that relations between the Bishop and the monks were uniformly poisonous. Strangely enough this does not seem to have been the case. We have seen already that the two sides co-operated in the freeing of John Drolle from servitude and the provision of the Austin Friars of Lynn with a supply of water.[59] In 1390 Bishop Henry was ready to help the cathedral sacrist by arbitrating over the Trinity-tide procession by the city clergy, whose performance had got out of hand.[60] Even more surprising is the fact that in or before 1395 he had made over to the Prior and convent his manor of Westhalle in Sedgeford, valued at £10 yearly. This he did without the proper licence from the King, which prompted an enquiry and an entry in the official records.[61] One does not usually hand over property to one's legal adversaries. Then, most of all, there is the warm tribute contained in the Bishop's epitaph, which must have been approved by the Prior at least, and has been preserved for us by John Capgrave, himself an Austin Friar of Lynn.[62]

Still more important evidence is to be found in the provision made in the will of that same Prior when, as the next Bishop of Norwich, he prepared for his own death some years later.[63] We are told that he required each of the professed monks to take it in turn, a week at a time, to celebrate mass daily in the cathedral at 6.00 a.m. in the chapel of St Mary the Virgin, in which he wished to be buried. During the service they were to intercede for his soul, the souls of his parents, his *parochiani* (perhaps his close colleagues and servants), Henry Despenser, his predecessor as bishop, and all the faithful departed. Why was Bishop Henry included? It does not seem to have been common form to include one's predecessor. Perhaps Totington may have felt that his old antagonist was more in need of prayer than most. But it is much more likely that there was an element of respect between the two men, even though they had been on opposite sides for so long.

Maybe, as time went on, enthusiasm for the controversy tended to diminish. Perhaps the stage had been reached when it was kept up simply because it was there, and Archbishop Arundel's award in 1411 was willingly accepted by all sides. If this were so an element of normality – even of co-operation – could well exist at a different level in areas where the legal dispute did not necessarily affect relationship. And, in any case, there may have been long periods when the conflict went off the boil, as it were, and the attitudes it engendered also receded into the background.

The last of the many controversies in which Henry Despenser became involved was quite different from any of the others. Potentially it was the most dangerous, indeed destructive, to his reputation as a bishop and as a man. The Clippesby Affair, as it is called, has been thoroughly examined by the late Roger Virgoe, so I need do little more than follow the account he has given.[64]

On 18 October 1390, Walter Cook of Little Plumstead, just to the east of Norwich, was killed at Great Plumstead nearby. It seems likely that he was a servant of the Bishop of Norwich. His widow, Juliana, accused Edmund Clippesby, of Little Plumstead, and his son, also Edmund, of her husband's murder. Both were outlawed: Edmund junior fled the country, and his father, while remaining, took care to place his possessions in the hands of trustees so that they could not be confiscated.

Edmund Clippesby was a well-known local lawyer. A veteran of about 70, he was retained as counsel by both the city and the cathedral priory of Norwich, with the latter of which Bishop Henry was in dispute. He had been steward of the Norfolk possessions of John of Gaunt, Duke of Lancaster, with whom the Bishop had been on bad terms since the time of the Flanders Crusade. He was not, therefore, *persona grata* with Despenser, quite apart from the murder of which he stood accused. Eventually, on 11 July 1392, a group of the Bishop's servants, led by Leonard Mallory, his esquire, went out to Little Plumstead, chased Clippesby through his house and into his garden, and there murdered him.[65]

Subsequently the Bishop supported his men openly in public places in the city of Norwich, and threatened various local knights and gentlemen in an effort to prevent them from bringing the matter to court.

Eventually, and inevitably, a royal commission was appointed to investigate both murders. Before this could convene, the local assize judges met and decided that the murder had been committed at the command of Bishop Despenser. The commission itself then heard various indictments, one or two of which agreed with the judges, while others took the less drastic view that the Bishop had maintained and comforted the murderers. But the matter was not to reach a conclusion. The whole case was recalled to chancery and eventually, on 10 December 1393, royal pardons were issued to all the accused at the request of Bishop Henry and his nephew Lord Thomas Despenser, then in high favour with Richard II. This of course amounted to a complete perversion of justice, particularly as it was not felt necessary to exonerate Henry himself.[66]

Clearly all kinds of undercurrents contributed to both murders. There was the rivalry between the Bishop and his Prior and convent, though it seems unlikely that the latter were implicated in any way. There was a local dispute in the Plumsteads over land. And at a much higher level local dignitaries were lining up behind Despenser and the court party of Richard II on the one hand, and the Lancastrian interest headed by John of Gaunt and his son Bolingbroke on the other – the same interest that Clippesby had once served.

But the crucial question is: did Bishop Henry tell, or encourage, Mallory and the rest to go and slay Clippesby? If so, one can hardly lay a more serious charge against a man in episcopal orders – or, indeed, any man. But it is also fair to say that the Bishop was sorely provoked. It was now getting on for two years since the murder of Walter Cook, and nothing, so far as one can gather, had been done to bring the Clippesbys to trial. Worse still, in spite of his outlawry, the elder Clippesby was still, so it appears, immune from any proceedings against him, probably feeling secure in the support of powerful backers, one of whom might even have been John of Gaunt himself. In this situation it would hardly have been surprising if Bishop Henry, not the most placid of men, had given vent to his anger and frustration in such a way that his servants, and especially Mallory, thought they could rely on his support if they hunted Clippesby down and put him to death. Indeed they appear to have been justified in holding this view, for their master certainly had a strong sense of loyalty, which would have made it unlikely that he would desert them even when they had done something as dreadful as that.

However we interpret the Clippesby Affair, it certainly marks the lowest point in Despenser's career. Even on the most favourable assessment he failed to show the restraint under provocation that is required of those in public life. Neither did he, in the long run, escape the consequences. As Roger Virgoe points out, the murder disgusted many people and so reinforced and hardened the pro-Lancastrian element in the diocese that, when Henry Bolingbroke usurped the throne in 1399, a shift of power occurred which effectively deprived Bishop Henry of his influence. He had to accept, albeit with a bad grace, the new state of affairs and the local supremacy of Sir Thomas Erpingham and his associates.

After the Clippesby Affair it seems impossible that when the Bishop died he should do so in the odour of sanctity. Yet he did; and it is not sufficient to say that some people have short memories. Often first impressions of an event are not lasting; and perhaps, as time went by, the misdeeds of the Clippesbys counted for more in popular memory than the highly irregular manner in which Edmund's life was brought to an end.

Notes

1. Register, F52V.
2. *Chronicon Angliæ*, ed. E. Maunde Thompson, Rolls Series, 1874, pp. 139-140.
3. I Kings, chapter 12, vv. 1-16.
4. H.B. Workman, *John Wyclif*, Oxford, 1926, vol. ii, p. 65.
5. *C.P.R.*, 1374-1377, p. 502.
6. Workman, op. cit., p. 65.
7. *C.Cl.R.*, 1377-1381, p. 85.
8. Workman, op. cit., p. 65.
9. D. M. Owen, *The Making of King's Lynn*, London, 1985, p. 417.
10. E.H. Goulburn, *A History of the See of Norwich*, London, 1876, p. 445.
11. Owen, op. cit., p. 34.
12. Ibid.
13. Owen, op. cit., p. 379. For the trouble in 1234, when Thomas Blundeville was bishop, see *English Episcopal Acta: Norwich 1213-1243*, ed. C. Harper-Bill, Appendix 11, no. 41A. (forthcoming, 1999)
14. Owen, op. cit., p. 416.
15. See above, p.30.
16. Workman, op. cit., p. 65.
17. Register, F52V.
18. K. McKisack, *The Fourteenth Century*, Oxford, 1959, pp. 376ff: E.F. Jacob, *The Fifteenth Century*, Oxford, 1961, p. 92.
19. *Chronicon Angliæ*, ut supra, p. 258.
20. I am grateful to Michael Yorke, now Dean of Lichfield, for helping my wife and I to see and photograph these misericords.

21. Owen, op. cit., p. 122.

22. *C.P.R.*, 1381-1385, p. 217.

23. *C.P.R.,* 1391-1396, p. 14.

24. Owen, op. cit., p. 135.

25. Ibid, pp. 135-139.

26. Ibid, p. 140.

27. *C.P.R.*, 1401-1405, p. 67.

28. See above, p.25.

29. *C.P.R.*, 1401-1405, p. 274.

30. M.D. Legge, (ed) *Anglo-Norman Letters and Petitions,* Oxford, 1941, no. 44, p. 92.

31. *C.P.R.*, 1401-1405, p. 307. For further details regarding the dispute with Lynn see below, pp. 129-30.

32. These two brasses are among the largest in England, but their design marks them out as imports from the Low Countries. Obviously the two mayors had seen specimens of this type while on business there and preferred them. The Braunche brass depicts the Peacock Feast which Mayor Braunche gave in honour of Edward III when he visited Lynn.

33. Register, F195R. (15 September, 1394) Problems between the Bishop of Norwich and Wymondham (not to mention the priory at Binham) went back a long way.

34. See Harper-Bill, op. cit., Appendix 11, no. 27. Walsingham's successor John Savage took his oath of obedience on 22 October, 1400. Dr John Darlington presided at the ceremony, Bishop Henry being away from the diocese. Register, F261V.

35. see note 33 above.

36. C. Fine. R., 1377-1383, p. 199. For the difficulties inherent in the job of collector see A.K. McHardy, 'The English Clergy and the Hundred Years War' in *Studies in Church History*[20], 1983, p. 172 and notes 9, 10 and 11.

37. *C. Fine. R.*, 1377-1383, pp. 207-208.

38. *Chronicon Angliæ,* ut supra, pp. 258-261. This also held good for the priors of other St Albans cells in Norwich diocese. Thomas Walsingham, *Ypodigma Neustriæ,* ed. H.T. Riley, Rolls Series, 1876, p. 331.

39. *Chronicon Angliæ,* pp. 258-259. Reference to the Bishop's youth would suggest that this diatribe was already in existence before Thomas Walsingham found himself in Bishop Henry's presence in 1394.

40. Register, F247R. *Chronique De La Traison et Mort de Richart Deux Roy D'Engleterre,* ed. B. Williams, London, 1846, p. 184.

41. *C. Fine. R.*, 1377-1383, p. 243.

42. Dom David Knowles, *The Religious Orders in England,* vol. ii, Cambridge, 1955, pp. 167-168. E.F. Jacob (op. cit., p. 300) says that Thetford had secured a papal bull granting freedom of election before 1376.

43. *C. Fine. R.*, 1377-1383, p. 208. This letter was written on the same day as the second rebuke to Bishop Henry over St Albans. cf. note 37.

44. *Norwich Cathedral, 1096-1996,* London and Rio Grande, 1996, p. 446.

45. Knowles, op. cit., ii, p. 58. For Easton see pp. 56-58 and for Brunton pp. 58-60. For the library see Knowles, ad. loc., and Norwich Cathedral, ut supra, pp. 332-338 (article by Barbara Dodwell).

46. Owen, op. cit., p. 122.

47. Register, F1R.

48. Register, F79R.

49. Register, F89R. This was issued at the port of Sandwich on 8 May, 1383.

50. Register, F90V, dated 26 June, 1383.

51. E.H. Carter, *Studies in Norwich Cathedral History,* Norwich, 1935, p. 37.

52. Norman Tanner, *The Church in Late Medieval Norwich,* Toronto, 1984, pp. 158-162.

53. Tanner, op. cit., p. 160.

54. *Calendar of Papal Letters, 1396-1404,* p. 11. Other stages of the dispute are referred to in *Calendar of Papal Letters, 1362-1396,* p. 525 (1395); *C.P.R., 1391-1396,* p. 712 (1396); *C.P.R., 1396-1399,* p. 107 (1397); *Calendar of Papal Letters, 1396-1404,* p. 273 (1400).

55. Carter, op. cit., p. 37. Nevill accuses the Bishop of having terrorised the monks for fifteen years. 'Nec domi pacatior quam foris fuit quippe qui monachis atrox inexpiabile bellum indiceret eosque omne jure antiquo ac libertate privare conatus sit adeo et per annos quindecim multis vexatos injuriis incredibiliter afflixerit. Diu tamen restiterunt monachi sed tamen forensi decertatione fracti ac debilitate omnis ille repugnandi fervor atque impetus ita refrixit ut eo demum deventum fuerit ut sponte quadringentas marcas antistiti dare consentirent.'

56. Carter, op. cit., p. 38.

57. Carter, op. cit., pp. 46-59 (Latin) and pp. 60-72 (English). Those who subscribed to the treaty included Sir Thomas Erpingham, Sir Robert Berney, Dr William Carleton and Master William Bakton.

58. Tanner, op. cit., p. 160. For the trouble over reverencialia in the time of Bishop Brown or Brouns (1436-1445) see *Norwich Cathedral,* ut supra, p. 298 and note 57, referring to an article on this bishop by E.F. Jacob.

59. See above, p.88.

60. See above, p.30.

61. *Calendar of Inquisitions Miscellaneous, 1392-1399,* no. 86, p. 41.

62. John Capgrave, *Liber De Illustribus Henricis,* ed. F. C. Hingeston, Rolls Series, 1858, p. 174.

63. Tanner, op. cit., p. 214.

64. Roger Virgoe, 'The Murder of Edmund Clippesby', in *Norfolk Archæology XXXV* (1973), pp. 302-307.

65. This was not the only occasion on which the Bishop's servants committed theft and grievous bodily harm. J. M., otherwise unidentified, writes to Henry to complain that Nicholas Stukle, his esquire, Geoffrey, one of his valets, and sixteen others, all armed, had broken into his house, dragged him out of it, wounded him and had stolen his sword, dagger and purse. Unlike Edmund Clippesby he survived, but only just. M.D. Legge, op. cit., no. 299, pp. 363-364.

66. Those pardoned were: William Whyteley, domestic servant of the said bishop:
        John Hunne:
        John Ferour:
        John Whyteley:
        John Madour:
        John Doget, 'barbour':
        John Cope, cook:
        John Braddeley alias Bradlee:
        Leonard Mallory alias Malore, esquire:
        Robert Bradlay:
        Peter atte Wode of Hoxne.
Apart from the last two these were all domestic servants of Bishop Despenser. *C.P.R., 1391-1396,* p. 341.

6. The Bishop and the Lollards

The quarrels and controversies reviewed in the last chapter all have to do with rights, privileges, relationships and prohibitions. They were not concerned with those higher spiritual matters to which the ministry of the Church is meant to relate above all else. Medieval bishops were consecrated to be guardians of the faith, which involved taking a lead in the detection of false teaching and the application of pastoral methods required to reconcile those who were led astray.[1] Soon after his appointment as Bishop of Norwich, Henry Despenser found himself, with many others, caught up in a controversy which shook the medieval Church to its foundations. The question being put was, 'are the doctrines and practice of the Western Church true?' And the answer from some quarters was emphatically in the negative.

The person responsible for this turmoil, which is sometimes given the name of the Premature Reformation, was an Oxford theologian called John Wyclif, who was born around 1320 and died in 1384.[2]

A Yorkshireman, Wyclif was an academic of prodigious learning and industry. He was not, however, endowed with a very attractive personality. He appears to have had a chip on his shoulder over the matter of ecclesiastical preferments he wanted but was not given, preferments that would have helped to ease his academic career at Oxford as similar gifts did for many others.

Wyclif and Bishop Henry were at Oxford at the same time. Both rented rooms at Queen's College, though neither, it would appear, was a member of the foundation. Henry stayed there when he returned to study at the end of his life. But it is highly doubtful that they were in any kind of contact. Wyclif may well have subscribed to the fashionable theologian's scorn for civil lawyers, which Henry and other aristocratic young clerks studying that discipline may have resented. But with the Bishop of Norwich one can never be certain. He had a serious side and a sharp intellect. When William Sawtry, soon to be the first Lollard martyr,[3] was examined at South Elmham, was it Henry's theological experts who put the questions on his behalf? Or was the Bishop himself competent enough to take a full part in the discussion?

In modern times political, social, economic or constitutional controversies in England are frequently enlivened by academic experts, who are called upon to give their opinions one way or the other. This technique was not unknown in the fourteenth century. As the Hundred Years War progressed, with results less and less satisfactory to the English, it was increasingly felt by the magnates and other leading laity that the Church, with its immense wealth and vast holdings of land, should play a much greater part in financing that war. Indeed, the most radical among them pressed for at least some of its endowments to be taken back altogether, on the grounds that in time of national emergency the Church should not expect to hold on to all the gifts made by pious folk from the national wealth in days of old. Those who took this view, among them John of Gaunt himself, found John Wyclif to be a very able advocate, to the extent that he was employed by the Crown as a *'peculiaris clericus'* (clerk with special duties), to be called on when required to argue on its behalf. For this he was given a retaining fee. But others argued too; and Wyclif was present at the Parliament of 1371 when two Augustinian friars took up the same cause. But it was a lay lord who maintained that 'when war breaks out we must take from the endowed clergy a portion of their temporal possessions, as property which belongs to us and the kingdom in common, and so wisely defend the country with property which exists among us in superfluity.' This was a very explosive issue, and Wyclif's thoughts on it were entirely secular.[4]

From attacking the Church on the financial front John Wyclif proceeded to consider some of its most cherished theological beliefs, together with the spiritual sanctions by which it maintained its pre-eminence. Here, of course, he was not putting forward new ideas, but was drawing upon the work of earlier doctors and divines like St Augustine, Robert Grosseteste, the thirteenth-century Bishop of Lincoln, and Richard FitzRalph, Archbishop of Armagh, who had died not long before in 1360. But in his hands, and following his theological investigations, the two main propositions that emerged struck at the heart of the medieval institutional Church.

The first of these was concerned with dominion and grace. Wyclif held that the exercise of all human authority depended on grace. Grace is defined as the possession of a right relationship with God. Should this relationship be lost through sin, all right to authority, and the possessions that go with it, is immediately forfeited. This led Wyclif, in Miss McKisack's words, 'to the specific conclusion that if an ecclesiastic abuse his property the secular power may deprive him; that popes and cardinals alike may err; that neither is essential to the true government of the Church, and that a worldly pope is a heretic who ought to be deposed'.[5] In contrast to this he held that everyone in a state of grace has true lordship.

Having questioned the institutional and hierarchical basis of the medieval Church, Wyclif then proceeded to attack one of its main theological bastions, the teaching regarding the eucharist, the blessed sacrament of Christ's body and blood. This made use of the current academic distinction between substance (the basic nature of a thing) and accidents (its outward shape and appearance). Traditional doctrine, defined by the Fourth Lateran Council in 1215, and later elaborated by St Thomas Aquinas, laid down that at the moment of consecration the bread and wine of the eucharist retained their accidents – in other words the outward appearance of bread and wine – but that the substance was changed into the actual body and blood of Christ. The accidents were retained so as to avoid the repugnance the faithful would experience otherwise.

This doctrine of transubstantiation, as it is called, Wyclif emphatically denied, though it is going too far to say that he substituted the 'real absence' for the real presence of Christ in the sacrament, in other words the contention that the Eucharist is purely symbolic. In his own words Christ is present 'not by way of multiplication, but virtually only, as a king is in every part of his kingdom'.[6] For him the substance of the bread and wine remained after consecration. But leaving theological subtleties aside, John Wyclif's action struck hard against the prestige of the priesthood, which was largely based on their power to 'make God' whenever they celebrated mass.

From 1377 these opinions attracted increasingly critical attention from church leaders.[7] For his part Wyclif did not hesitate to proclaim his opinions from the London pulpits. In that same year Pope Gregory XI censured eighteen of Wyclif's propositions submitted to him by his opponents, but for some time the reformer remained secure, benefiting from the support of John of Gaunt and Joan, Princess of Wales on the one hand, and the university authorities at Oxford on the other. Matters came to a head in 1379, when he delivered the lectures embodying his views on the eucharist. But even then a council of Oxford theologians, faced with twelve propositions derived from those lectures, pronounced against them by only a narrow majority. Wyclif, greatly distressed by this verdict, decided to appeal to the King rather than to any academic or ecclesiastical body, thus giving further proof of his Erastian preference for the secular power.

What finally undid John Wyclif was the Peasants' Revolt and its consequences. There is no proof that Wyclif and his doctrines played any real part in stirring up the rebels, but it was his misfortune to fall foul of the reactionary forces that prevailed after the revolt was crushed.

Having succeeded the murdered archbishop of Canterbury the year before, William Courtenay saw that the time had come to deal with the arch-heretic. So in May 1382 a synod of theologians was convened at the convent of the Black Friars in London. This considered twenty-four propositions extracted from Wyclif's writings, and after debating for four days it condemned them all unanimously. Whereas in earlier times Wyclif had received much support from the four orders of friars, orchestrated by John of Gaunt, those at the Black Friars synod now turned against him and endorsed the condemnation. He was not put on trial – his powerful protectors saw to that – but he was forbidden to preach or teach at Oxford. Retiring to his rectory at Lutterworth he resisted failing health, and poured out a stream of polemical publications, which show that the adverse verdict at the Black Friars had not influenced him at all. Supported by his secretary and right hand man, John Purvey, he continued thus until his death on 31 December, 1384.

Having exiled Wyclif from Oxford, Archbishop Courtenay now moved against his leading supporters, Nicholas Hereford, John Aston and Philip Repingdon. In spite of obstruction from the university authorities, which was quickly crushed, the three were condemned. But by the end of the century all had recanted and embraced orthodoxy. Nicholas Hereford became Chancellor of Hereford Cathedral, and Repingdon ended his days as a well-approved bishop of Lincoln, having also served as abbot of his monastery at Leicester. From then on clergy of lesser ability are found leading the Lollard movement, with the help of a considerable number of able and devoted laity.

But just how strong was Lollardy in England during the last quarter of the fourteenth century and the opening years of the fifteenth? One contemporary is on record as saying that it had the support of half or more of the kingdom.[8] But until recently it was held that its adherents included only a very few of the upper classes, men usually described as the Lollard Knights.[9] Now, however, following the researches of Margaret Aston, Anne Hudson and Michael Wilks,[10] a very different picture has emerged. It is asserted that the government of the time at least countenanced, and sometimes openly supported, Wyclif, his ideas and his adherents, and that to hold royalist views involved theological as well as financial attitudes highly critical of the Church of Rome. Wilks goes so far as to say that:

'to see Wyclif and his movement in perspective one needs to see them against the background of a kingdom which had already largely negated papal power in practice, and had to all intents and purposes come to see itself as an autonomous national church. That this, from a strictly hierocratic standpoint, made it a kingdom of heretics can hardly be in doubt. As Gordon Leff has put it, what distinguished heresy from mere dissent or heterodoxy was not simple disagreement about the content of the faith, but the practical political error of refusing to submit to ecclesiastical authority. Heresy was not deviation from the faith so much as deviation from the faith as defined and authorised by the Roman church. On this basis it is simply not true that there was no widescale heresy in England before 1380: it was so heretical that everyone had to pretend that it wasn't.'[11]

Another, and equally revolutionary, point is that Wyclif sought to effect his reformation from the top downwards rather than from the bottom upwards.[12]

Generations of students have become familiar with the idea of Lollard 'poor preachers' with russet gowns and bare feet spreading Wyclif's ideas among humble folk who had become profoundly dissatisfied with an unreformed and over-powerful Church, and who sought for something simpler and more akin to the teachings of holy scripture and the life of the primitive Church. They have realised the great impetus given to this by the publication of the Lollard Bible in a language people could read or have read to them. But all the time Wyclif was pinning his faith on the support of the aristocracy and the upper classes, whose example could ensure that those under their control were reached with the new doctrines and would give them their support.[13]

Nevertheless, the coming of these new ideas about Wyclif and Lollardy brings with it a certain difficulty. It is easy to assume that in the late fourteenth century people were either Lollards or anti-Lollards, reformers or Catholics. But in the days of Wyclif and Henry Despenser there was no such polarisation. Many who made discreet use of Lollard devotional material, which was plentiful, remained in all essentials devout Catholics. Great men like Thomas of Woodstock owned, and presumably used, a Lollard Bible. The Lollard Knights had a reputation for austerity, but they certainly did not turn their backs on the cultured sophistication of the court in which they lived. Sir John Clanvowe, for instance, could write a love poem as well as *The Two Ways*, a noted devotional treatise.[14] Furthermore, these knights did not subscribe to the pacifism some other Lollards fervently espoused, and had service in the field to prove it. Sir John Montagu was crusading with the Teutonic Knights in Lithuania by 1391, and was regarded by Walsingham as the most heretical of all the knights. Sir Lewis Clifford was evidently skilled in knightly pursuits, for he played a prominent part in the celebrated tournament at St Inglevert, near Calais, where three French knights challenged all comers.[15] On the contrary, many devoted and orthodox church-people were attracted to certain Lollard beliefs without embracing the whole package, while a significant number of mainstream Catholics, monks included, abominated the Flanders Crusade and its leader with the same disgust as contemporary Lollard pamphleteers and sermonisers, who took their lead from Wyclif himself.[16]

Into this highly complex jigsaw we must now endeavour to fit Henry Despenser.

Without doubt he was one of the leaders of what Wilks calls the hierocratic party, bishops who supported papal as against royal supremacy.[17] It could hardly be otherwise, for the promotion of this outstanding soldier-clerk was at the direct initiative of Urban V, and had to be ratified, as we have seen, by his repudiation of anything in the appointment process that might be repugnant to English law. Brinton of Rochester was another diocesan bishop who comes into

106

this category, though the two contemporary archbishops of Canterbury, Courtenay and Arundel, also took a strong line against Wyclif and all his works. It might almost be said that if Courtenay had not shown exemplary energy and ability in the early 1380s the premature reformation might well have become actual and irreversible.

By contrast other bishops took a more royalist line and, conscious of the prevailing attitudes at court, their reaction to heresy was correspondingly more relaxed, a point that was not lost on Thomas Walsingham.

Despite his critical comments on other matters the great chronicler has nothing but praise for the way in which Bishop Henry faced the challenge of widespread heresy. He writes that unlike the other bishops, who shamefully neglected their people, Henry refused to allow his flock to be polluted, for which Walsingham calls down blessings on his head for evermore.

'He swore, moreover, and did not repent of what he said, that if anyone belonging to that perverse sect should presume to preach in his diocese, they would be taken to the fire or beheaded. Consequently, having understood this, no one belonging to that tendency had any desire to embrace martyrdom, with the result that, up to now, the faith and true religion have remained unaffected within the bounds of his episcopal authority.'[18]

In another of his works the same writer invokes the Roman poet Martial in his praise of the Bishop: *'temporibus malis ausus est esse bonum'* – in evil times he dared to be good.[19] Here, surely, is strong justification for Hudson and Wilks' thesis regarding the real power of Lollardy in late fourteenth-century England.

Of course these things could be, and indeed have been, expressed very differently. In the nineteenth century Dean Goulburn embroidered Walsingham's words by stating that any Lollard found in Despenser's diocese should 'either hop headless or fry a faggot'.[20] Assuming the accuracy of Walsingham's account, there can be no doubt that in 1397 the Bishop was wholeheartedly in favour of the petition calling for death by burning to be visited on all obdurate heretics.[21] But it is equally true that not a single Lollard was deprived of his life during Henry's tenure of the bishopric of Norwich. His colourful language, together with the force of his personality, seem to have kept heresy at bay until after his death. At first sight the fate of William Sawtry may seem to disprove this. Undoubtedly he was a native of the diocese, and having held posts at St Margaret, Lynn and at Tilney not far away, he was reported to the Bishop for heresy. After examination at South Elmham[22] and a spell in custody he solemnly abjured his errors at Lynn in the episcopal presence. But having removed himself to London, where he became parish priest of St Osyth in Walbrook, he offended again, and as a relapsed heretic he went to the stake. As

107

this happened within the jurisdiction of the Bishop of London, Bishop Henry had no direct part in Sawtry's death, only an indirect one in that, like the other bishops, he had pressed for the death penalty to be imposed.

Nevertheless Bishop Henry did not always have to act on his own initiative. On 30 September, 1388, in common with all the other bishops, he and the Bishop of Lincoln were ordered to confiscate all manuscripts containing the heresies of Masters John Wyclif, Nicholas Hereford, John Aston and others. They were to make proclamation prohibiting anyone, under pain of total forfeiture, from maintaining or teaching such opinions, or causing books containing them to be written, bought or sold. Those who had such books were to surrender them, and after proclamation all offenders were to be committed to the nearest gaol until they had retracted their errors.[23] What should happen if they failed to do so had not yet been worked out. By 1401, with the enactment of *De Hæretico Comburendo*, it was.

This seems unusual conduct for a government and court where Wyclif and his opinions were, according to Wilks, in such high favour. But in 1388 the Lords Appellant, sworn enemies of misgovernment and corruption in high places, were in firm control of the country, and another plank in their programme appears to have been the re-establishment of orthodoxy in alliance with the hierocratic clergy, of whom Despenser was one.[24] Therefore they lost no time in using the machinery of government to deal with Wyclif's supporters in the various dioceses, much to the Bishop's satisfaction. One gathers from this that political changes and shifts of power at the centre could make a considerable difference to Wyclif's success in spreading his doctrines.

As for the Flanders Crusade it has already been explained that Wyclif and the Lollards were for the most part strongly opposed to the whole enterprise and its leader in particular. But was the crusade affected by this in any way? For example, did John of Gaunt and Thomas of Woodstock hold back from leading a relief expedition to Flanders because, on religious grounds, they felt such a crusade to be totally flawed? To think so is probably far-fetched, as Gaunt already had reasons to refuse to help the man who had so seriously upset his own plans by gaining the ear of Parliament in 1382/3. But in the case of another leader, Sir William Beauchamp, there is more convincing evidence.

We already know that, although destined for the priesthood, he had given up the idea in favour of a military career. Why was that? He certainly remained devout, and is numbered among those very close to the leading Lollard Knights, whether actually of their company or not. Serious-minded he undoubtedly was, for he was one of the advocates of devotion to the Holy Name of Jesus, a cult which could embrace without difficulty orthodox and Lollard alike. Against this, when Captain of Calais, he is said to have been a supporter of the Lords

Appellant, who stood with the more papalist bishops against Wycliffite tendencies at court.[25]

The fall of Richard II and his court party in 1399 was a severe blow to the would-be reformers. Wycliffite programmes and ideas lost their authority and backing, though the new King did not send away or dismiss all who were of that tendency. His support of Sir John Cheyne is a case in point,[26] and Archbishop Arundel had occasion to complain about the lack of respect with which the king's household treated the eucharist.[27] But support for Lollard ideas finally drained away with the failure of the rising led by Sir John Oldcastle (Shakespeare's model for Falstaff) in 1413, and the accession, a little earlier that year, of a king, Henry V, of unimpeachable orthodoxy. From then onwards Lollardy became what it has always been thought to be, a movement of the poorer classes and humble, obscure, clergy.

By that time, of course, Bishop Henry had been dead for several years, but his repressive measures had been so successful that active persecution of Lollards in the diocese of Norwich did not begin until the episcopate of John Wakering, who was bishop between 1415 and 1425. Even then Lollardy seems to have had little hold on Norwich itself, a fact Norman Tanner attributes to popular satisfaction with the Church as it then was.[28]

But, for all Bishop Henry's vigilance, the diocese of Norwich is known to have harboured two other active Lollard sympathisers beside the ill-fated William Sawtry. Some would maintain that there were three, the other being Richard Caister, Vicar of St Stephen in the city of Norwich. He died in 1420 and his reputation was such that he had been visited by the formidable Margery Kempe of Lynn.[29] Caister was without doubt a conspicuously saintly man, in whose honour a strong unofficial cult grew up.[30] The evidence for Lollard sympathies is, however, very weak, pointing out nothing more than the absence of stock phrases of an orthodox nature in his will.

No such disclaimer can be made for Sir Lewis Clifford, whom we have seen presenting a relative to the rectory of Haddiscoe.[31] K. B. Mcfarlane[32] has no hesitation in numbering him among the knights of the later fourteenth century whose Lollard sympathies are clearly revealed when investigated. For example, the attitude of these knights towards the blessed sacrament was clearly not orthodox. They kept their hats on in its presence, for which reason they came to be called the Hooded Knights. One of their number, Sir John Montagu, even refused to receive the sacrament as he faced death by lynching at the hands of the townsfolk of Cirencester in 1400.[33] According to Walsingham,[34] Clifford abandoned his Lollard beliefs in 1402, when they were becoming increasingly unfashionable and even dangerous.

Nevertheless, when he drew up his will in September, 1404, he described

109

himself as false and a traitor, unworthy to be called a Christian man.[35] Does this mean that he regretted his recantation in 1402, or, conversely, that he deplored his departure from orthodoxy for so many years? But in any case his self-loathing is typical of Lollard wills of the period, which often use extravagant phrases like 'foul carrion' to describe the testator's body or corpse.

Although his position must have been well-known no action was ever taken against Clifford by the church authorities, including Bishop Henry, presumably because his position at a court where Lollardy was viewed favourably could have given him ample protection.

The other major problem confronting Bishop Henry was the notorious William Northwold. He first appears in September 1380, when he is in trouble for uttering threats against Hugh Gaudeby, Archdeacon of Sudbury, the archdeacon's official and other ministers.[36] On this occasion he managed to obtain his freedom, as he did again in 1384 when accused of planning to go abroad to commit acts prejudicial to the king and the realm.[37] In 1386, having presumably become reconciled with Gaudeby, he enters into financial arrangements with him. On one occasion the two men bind themselves to each other in recognisances of £1000, a truly enormous sum in those days.[38] One wonders why. Later in the same year, Northwold, described as Master, appears as an aggrieved party and is said to be Archdeacon of Sudbury. But the statement given by Mcfarlane that he is supposed to have held office for seven years seems impossible to substantiate, as other men are known to have held the archdeaconry in 1380 (Hugh Gaudeby), 1384 (John Lincoln and Hugh Sturmy), 1387 (Hugh Sturmy again), and 1389 (Thomas Hethersett).[39] To add to the difficulties Northwold is described as parson of Timworth, a village just to the north of Bury St Edmunds, in 1380[40] while in 1390 he holds part of the church of West Walton far away in the Fens. He is then freed from the threat of outlawry hanging over him for failing to answer Bishop Henry concerning a debt of £24.[41] Finally, 'for needful and notable causes nearly moving the king', he is strictly forbidden to preach or teach anywhere in the realm under pain of imprisonment or forfeiture.[42]

Here, then, we have a man with a dubious reputation in financial matters (and probably not only those) who has to be prevented from preaching in England and doing the country harm abroad. What is the explanation? It seems that he has become, or has appeared to become, a Lollard.

As such he figures in Mcfarlane's pages[43] as one of a group of heretics resident in Northampton. These were given aid and comfort by John Fox, the mayor, whose attitude was bitterly opposed by a merchant named Richard Stormsworth. As part of his campaign Stormsworth made an outspoken attack on William Northwold. Among other things he accuses him of simony, on the proceeds of which 'he liveth deliciously at this time in the house of St Andrew at Northampton, where he hath caused such debate between the prior and monks that the house is well-nigh undone, and many of the monks fled away'. This, adds Stormsworth, has happened at other religious houses at which Northwold has previously lodged. 'His whole conversation', continues the outraged merchant, 'as well in the court of Rome as in England hath been in simony and subtle dealing, who notwithstanding is still in Northampton amongst the Lollards and misbelievers reputed a prophet speaking with the tongue of an angel'.

To cap it all, at a confrontation on 9 March, 1393, Northwold had dressed himself up in the robes of a doctor of divinity, 'whereas he never took any degree in schools'.

For those who live in modern times this is a familiar story; but in the 1390s only a blunt, no-nonsense merchant could see through the web of duplicity and brainwashing Northwold had so subtly woven around him. In fact he is clearly visible as a medieval example of a religious charlatan like Molière's Tartuffe, mesmerising his disciples by his eloquence and apparent piety, while making sure of a good living. In the circumstances it is quite possible that Stormsworth failed to substantiate his accusations, especially as his own motives were not entirely disinterested. But one certainly doubts the sincerity of Northwold's Lollard convictions. Confidence tricksters like him can turn any set of propositions to their own use regardless of whether they have any genuine belief in them or not.

How much, one wonders, did Henry Despenser know about all this? He would certainly have been aware of Northwold's early history in the diocese, and whether he really was an archdeacon or not. His friend Hugh Gaudeby was also close to the Bishop himself, particularly during a legal battle with the king as to who should present to the archdeaconry of Sudbury.[44] It also seems likely that he was cognisant of the later events at Northampton, although they happened well away from his diocese. For on 23 October 1404 he instituted Thomas Stormsworth, priest, to the living of Acle between Norwich and Great Yarmouth.[45] As the world is not full of Stormsworths, and medieval spelling is anything but exact, it seems likely that Thomas was related to Richard; and that we see here an expression of the Bishop's gratitude to the man who unmasked the slippery William Northwold so effectively. If so, it would have been entirely in character.

Notes

1. Guardianship of the faith remains the responsibility of bishops consecrated today, be they Orthodox, Anglican or Roman Catholic. The way in which they carry out the task will of course vary from tradition to tradition.

2. The literature on Wyclif is voluminous. The study by H. B. Workman (*John Wyclif*, 2 vols., Oxford, 1926) is largely superseded, but a good introduction is given by M. McKisack, *The Fourteenth Century*, Oxford, 1959, especially pages 510-517. See also p. 290.

3. The word Lollard probably comes from the Middle Dutch *lollærd*, a mumbler of prayers. (McKisack, op. cit., p. 517, note 3.)

4. McKisack, op. cit., pp. 290, 511. The speech from the 1371 parliament, given by Wyclif, is worthy of reproduction in full. (Workman, op. cit., book 2, chapter 9, pp. 210-211: *Wyclif, De civili dominio*, ii, p. 7.)

'Once upon a time thee was a meeting of many birds – among them was an owl. But the owl had lost her feathers, and made as though she suffered much from the frost. So she begged the other birds with a trembling voice to give her some of their feathers. They sympathised with her, and every bird gave the owl a feather, till she was overladen with strange feathers in unlovely fashion. Scarcely was this done when a hawk came in sight in quest of prey. Then the birds, to escape from the attacks of the hawk, demanded their feathers back again from the owl, and on her refusal each of them took back his own feather by force, and so escaped the danger, while the owl remained more miserably unfledged than before. Even so, when war breaks out we must take from the endowed clergy a portion of their temporal possessions, as property which belongs to us and the kingdom in common, and so wisely defend the country with property which exists among us in superfluity.'

5. McKisack, op. cit., p. 512.

6. *Oxford Dictionary of the Christian Church*, ed. F. L. Cross, Oxford, 1958, p. 1480. One wonders what he would have made of the classical definition we owe to Elizabeth I, which combines devotion to the sacrament with a refusal to make a precise definition of what actually happens to the elements at consecration.

'His was the word that spake it;
He took the bread and brake it;
And what that word doth make it
I do believe and take it.'

7. For the following section I have drawn extensively on McKisack, op. cit., 512-515.

8. *Chronicon Henrici Knighton, Monachi Leycestrensis*, ed. J. R. Lumby, Rolls Series, 1895, vol. 2, p. 185. A new edition of this chronicle has just appeared, edited and translated by Geoffrey Martin, Oxford, 1996.

9. Knights thought to belong to this group include Thomas Latimer, John Trussell, Lewis Clifford, John Pecche, Richard Stury, Reginald Hilton, William Neville, John Clanvowe, John Montagu. (McKisack, op. cit., p. 521, notes 1 and 2.) William Beau-champ may also have been implicated.

10. Anne Hudson, *The Premature Reformation*, Oxford, 1988: Michael Wilks, *Royal Priesthood: the origins of Lollardy in The Church in a changing society*. Publications of the Swedish Society of Church History, new series 30, Uppsala, 1978, pp. 63-69.

11. Wilks, op. cit., p. 69.

12. In this, of course, he was right. That is how the Reformation eventually came about in the sixteenth century.

13. Wilks, op. cit., pp. 65-66.

14. Wilks, op. cit., p. 65.

15. McKisack, op. cit., p. 521 (Montagu): Froissart, *Chronicles*, translated and edited by G. Brereton, Harmondsworth, 1968, p. 380 (Clifford).

16. Ibid, p. 431 and note 3.

17. Wilks, op. cit., p. 67.

18. Walsingham, *Historia Anglicana*, vol. 2, p. 189 (writer's translation).

19. Walsingham, *Ypodigma Neustriæ*, ed. H. T. Riley, Rolls Series, 1876, pp. 359-360.

112

20. E. H. Goulburn, *A History of the See of Norwich,* London, 1876, p. 454.

21. McKisack, op. cit., p. 522.

22. The manor house where the examination took place still exists.

23. *C.P.R.,* 1385-1389, p. 550. See H. G. Richardson, 'Heresy and the Lay Power under Richard II' in *English Historical Review,* 51 (1936), pp. 1-28. An earlier attempt to tighten up the procedure against heretics had been made in 1382. (ibid, p. 8)

24. Henry was, in fact, made a member of the Council in 1388, so he was carrying out a policy he himself had helped to formulate. (Froissart, *Chronicles,* ed. Kervyn de Lettenhove, Brussels, 1870-1877, vol. 12, p. 259.)

25. Hudson, op. cit., p. 430: McKisack, op. cit., p. 355.

26. Hudson, op. cit., p. 113. In 1399 Cheyne resigned from the Speakership of the Commons, probably after opposition from Archbishop Arundel on the grounds of his Lollard sympathies. In 1404 he again clashed with Arundel at the parliament in Coventry, when he supported a move to confiscate the temporalities of the Church.

27. Ibid.

28. N. Tanner, *The Church in Late Medieval Norwich 1370-1532,* Toronto, 1984, p. 165.

29. *The Book of Margery Kempe,* translated by B. A. Windeatt, Harmondsworth, 1985, pp. 74-76, 186.

30. Tanner, op. cit., p. 163. In 1994 a medallion pertaining to his cult came up for auction and was bought, on the writer's recommendation, for the Castle Museum at Norwich.

31. Above, p.30.

32. K. B. Mcfarlane, *Lancastrian Kings and Lollard Knights,* Oxford, 1972, passim and pp. 161, 164, 174, 178, 210.

33. Ibid, p. 208, from Walsingham, *Historia Anglicana,* vol. 2, p. 244.

34. Walsingham, *Historia Anglicana,* vol. 2, pp. 252-253.

35. McKisack, op. cit., p. 521, note 2.

36. *C.CL.R.,* 1377-1381, p. 469.

37. *C.CL.R.,* 1381-1385, p. 595.

38. *C.CL.R.,* 1385-1389, pp. 125, 134.

39. *C.CL.R.,* 1377-1381, p. 469: *C.P.R.,* 1381-1385, pp. 408, 458: Register, FF.124R-V: *C.P.R.,* 1388-1392, p. 25: and Register, F.137V.

40. *C.CL.R.,* 1377-1381, p. 469.

41. *C.P.R.,* 1388-1392, p. 68.

42. *C.CL.R.,* 1396-1399, p. 102.

43. K. B. Mcfarlane, *John Wyclif and the Beginnings of English Nonconformity,* English Universities Press, 1952, pp. 141-142. See also Hudson, op. cit., pp. 79-80 and 153. Fox was even able to frustrate the officials of the Bishop of Lincoln in their efforts to prevent Northwold from preaching.

44. *C.P.R.,* 1385-1389, p. 585.

45. Register F.310R.

7. The Ageing Bishop (1383-1406)

After the failure of the Flanders Crusade it might have been expected that the fighting Bishop of Norwich would fight no more. He had suffered a very hard blow; but paradoxically military activity may have helped to revive his spirits. When we say that he was a fighting bishop this does not, of course, imply that he involved himself in the melée like an ordinary knight or man-at-arms. He may have done so, briefly, at North Walsham, but in Flanders his rôle was that of a commander. In any case, the battle of Dunkirk was won so thoroughly by the English archers that little activity may have been required of anyone else. But as the years went by, it is likely that Henry still sought, and responded to, the company of other soldiers, and in the years following the Flanders Crusade there were times when this was not difficult to obtain.

The first of these came in 1385, when he had still not recovered his temporalities. John of Gaunt's attempts to make peace with Scotland, leaving him free to pursue his own interests in Spain, had been rudely overturned by the French. They felt that the time had come to invade England, thus avenging the misery that had been heaped on their country during the last forty years. To this end a small force had been dispatched to Scotland in 1384, followed by a much larger one, under the celebrated admiral Jean de Vienne, in the following year. This was intended to reinforce their Scottish allies, in concert with a large-scale invasion of England from the south.[1]

To such a threat an immediate response was imperative, and a large army was raised. Parliament had already supplied ample financial support, though it had in mind a royal invasion of France. The reality was to be quite different from that.

As the great host moved northwards the Bishop of Norwich left his see city on or just after 17 July[2] and joined it two or three days later. At once he was given a prominent position in the vanguard. According to the *Westminster Chronicler,* he was accompanied by his crusading banner (the Scots, like the French, supported the antipope and were therefore schismatics) and, from Durham onwards, by the famous standard of St Cuthbert, which was entrusted to him by the monks of the cathedral.[3] The vanguard was in fact commanded by John of Gaunt, but there seems to have been no friction between him and Bishop Henry on this occasion.

Other friction there undoubtedly was. Things started badly when the King's half-brother John Holland, notorious for his violent behaviour, killed the heir of the Earl of Stafford in a brawl. Richard was furious, threatening the murderer with punishment as a common criminal. Indeed the death of his mother Joan,

114

the Fair Maid of Kent, is said to have been caused by the enmity between her sons. Having at last crossed the border, the army burnt the abbeys of Melrose and Newbattle, and eventually entered Edinburgh. But they found no Scots or French to fight, some having retreated to the north, while the main army, under Jean de Vienne, evaded them and marched via the western road to Carlisle. When John of Gaunt suggested that the English army should spend time pillaging the countryside beyond the river Forth, he was confronted by his angry and petulant nephew, who announced that he was tired of the whole enterprise and was going home. Worse still, he added various pointed remarks about his uncle's indifferent success as a general. Scarcely a fortnight after entering Scotland the army passed Berwick on its way home, having nothing but devastation to its credit. As for Jean de Vienne and his Frenchmen, dislike of Scottish living conditions prevailed where English arms could not. After creating havoc in Cumberland they gratefully returned home to a more congenial civilisation.[4]

What did Bishop Henry make of all this? In any dispute between the King and John of Gaunt it is clear enough which side he would take, on the basis of previous experience. But could he suppress the doubts that would have arisen when he beheld his sovereign behaving in a foolish and unkingly manner, egged on by his favourite De Vere? Loyalty has much to commend it, but Henry's loyalty was pledged more than once on behalf of people, low as well as high, who were totally unworthy of it. He was not a par-ticularly good judge of men, though he seems to have been better with clergy than with laity.

Disgusted by Richard's behaviour, John of Gaunt was eager to set sail with his expedition to Spain where, in English eyes at least, he was now King of Castile and Léon. But it was hardly a propitious moment. Ominous news came from just across the Channel of preparations for a French invasion of England – preparations on an immense scale.[5] There were even the walls of a pre-fabricated town expertly made of wood. This construction was designed to provide a secure base after a landing, and could be taken apart and moved from place to place as required. Nothing, it would seem, had been forgotten.

Froissart goes into much detail about this, but he also mentions the plans made in England to resist the invasion. Very sensibly the landing would be unopposed, and the French would be allowed to penetrate well inland before their ships, supplies and coastal base were attacked and their retreat effectively cut off. 'Only then,' he says, 'would they [the English] tackle the French army, not yet to fight a battle but as a harassing operation. The French would not be able to go foraging, nor would they find anything because the open country would all have been laid waste, and England is a bad country to campaign through on horseback. So they would be starved and in a desperate position.'[6]

Although it was not the most vulnerable area, East Anglia shared fully in

115

these defensive preparations. Commissions of array to raise troops were issued, some rather late in the day, for one, directed to the Bishop of Norwich, the bailiffs of Norwich and other named individuals, is dated 12 December 1386, at about the same time as the French postponed the operation indefinitely.[7] Rather earlier, various persons were commissioned to investigate the activities of armourers who, taking advantage of the danger of invasion, charged exorbitant prices for weapons, armour and horses. To back up these measures the King wrote to the citizens of Norwich, ordering them to fortify their city, array their men and look after their towers, gates and walls. As a postscript he asked for a loan of five hundred marks. In response, the citizens chose Bishop Henry as their governor and commander, with an advisory committee of eight to support him.[8]

But he did not confine his attention to Norwich. If the French were to come, Yarmouth would be in even greater danger, and extensive measures were taken to fortify and defend it. Sir Henry Percy, later to be known as Harry Hotspur, was sent there with 300 men-at-arms and 600 archers.[9] Difficulty arose, however, because ships from Yarmouth, with their crews, were urgently needed to go to London and operate from there whenever a threat developed. The plan was that men from the neighbouring villages should be drafted in to defend the port in place of the absent seamen. But some at least of the seamen did not want to be away from their home town at such a time of emergency, for the king's representatives were having great difficulty in enforcing his will.[10]

At the same time a strong commission, including the Bishop, leading knights of the area, and the bailiffs of Yarmouth, was hard at work directing the upgrading of the town's defences 'against imminent peril of the King's enemies'. True to form, however, Henry had gone ahead with a plan of his own, without referring to his colleagues.

In those days the areas of East and West Flegg were considered to be islands separate from the rest of Norfolk, and at the three ferries connecting them with the mainland he caused 'bastides' to be constructed. Presumably they were bastions or forts of some kind; the word is not being used to denote a carefully-planned fortified town of the kind built by both French and English in the disputed areas of south-west France. Whatever they were, the Bishop was exacting contributions from the local people to pay for them, and a decree of *Supersedeas Omnino* (stop everything) had to be issued.[11] But it is not harshly worded. Bishop Henry's activity is clearly appreciated, but the Council feels that the construction of these bastides will not be helpful at the present time. Furthermore, he should not have used a royal commission to carry out other defensive works as a pretext for putting his own ideas into practice. Strategically, of course, the situation turned on whether the French, if they came, would want to concern themselves with Flegg anyway.

In any case the French did not come. Their enormous preparations were not matched by decisiveness in the higher command. Various annoying mishaps and delays occurred, not to mention unhelpful weather, and when December came the great expedition was still waiting. At this point the Duke of Berry successfully advised against starting a campaign in winter, and amidst grumbling and recrimination the whole enterprise was stood down and the troops dispersed. The French taxpayers had reason to grumble, too, for Froissart estimates that they had needed to find over three million francs.[12]

With the benefit of hindsight we can see that the danger from a French invasion was effectively over by the end of 1386. But in England invasion fever did not die down for some time. In 1387, as we have seen, Bishop Henry had his manor houses of North Elmham and Gaywood crenellated so that they might serve as strong points in case of attack.[13]

The Bisop's manor house at North Elmham
Reconstruction and drawing by David Yaxley

As with the plans of Napoleon and Hitler centuries later, the sea was the biggest obstacle the French had to overcome. In 1386 it needed no help from any English fleet. When the Constable of France, coming from Brittany with seventy-two ships laden with men and supplies, attempted to join the rest of the invasion force, his fleet was scattered by a gale. Several of his ships were driven into the Thames, including one or two carrying components of the pre-fabricated town, together with the carpenters who made it. Others were wrecked off Zealand, and the Constable and the lords with him only reached Sluys after much difficulty and danger.[14]

But it was still fortunate for the English that the best soldier they boasted at the time could also function as an admiral. Richard Fitzalan, Earl of Arundel, was anxious to take the offensive against the French as they prepared their

117

invasion, and in December 1386 he agreed to serve the King with 2,500 men for three months from the beginning of March 1387. By 13 March he had all the men he needed, together with 60 ships. Ten days later he captured an enemy vessel, and learned that a great Flemish fleet was approaching. On the 27 March, battle was joined. The disparity in the size of the fleets was lessened when seventy Dutch and German ships changed sides because of a quarrel between the Flemish admiral and the French marshal. Furthermore, the Flemish ships lacked the men-at-arms they should have been carrying. Nevertheless, Arundel's victory was a superb achievement; and it became even more popular at home when, by order of the Council, between 8,000 and 9,000 tuns of wine, captured during the engagement, were sold off at a fraction of their normal price. This, as we are told, was almost as much as was imported into England in a normal year.[15]

According to Froissart, Bishop Henry was a member of Arundel's expedition.[16] But he could not have been present at the battle, as he was still at North Elmham on 27 March, when John Darlington was made Archdeacon of Norwich.[17] From that date, however, there is a gap in his register until 15 April, so he would have had time to join Arundel as he followed up his victory. The latter had already dealt a decisive blow at any attempt to resurrect the invasion and, as Palmer points out, he gave the Flemings further cause for discontent with their French prince and his French policies. Unfortunately, having arrived at Sluys, Arundel contented himself with some very profitable pillage when, by moving to capture the town, he could have dominated West Flanders for as long as he could keep his fleet together. He might even have encouraged Ghent to come out into the open and declare for England. As it was, so Froissart tells us, the pillage gained him 200,000 francs, more than the cost of the whole expedition. Bishop Henry might have reflected that if he had not been so intent on commanding the Flanders Crusade himself, the gifted but intemperate Arundel might have made a considerable – even decisive – difference to its fortunes.[18]

Nevertheless Henry's friendship with Arundel and his brother brought him many benefits. For Richard's younger brother, Thomas, was Bishop of Ely and destined to become Archbishop of Canterbury. More stable and level-headed than Richard, and possessed of exceptional ability, there were no complaints when he went to Ely at the age of only twenty, and it was he who won Henry back his temporalities. Walsingham tells the story well. Arundel's request for their restoration was bitterly opposed by the Chancellor, Michael de la Pole, Earl of Suffolk and an old antagonist of Bishop Henry. The Earl pointed out that these temporalities were worth £1,000 a year. So why, he demanded, should the government let them go? 'If you are so worried about the King's

118

interests suffering' countered Arundel, 'why were you so ready to take an annual grant of 1,000 marks when he made you Earl of Suffolk?' 'To this,' says Walsingham, 'the Earl could find nothing to say.'[19] Game, set and match to Arundel.

It seems likely that soon afterwards Henry was able, in some measure, to return the compliment by supporting the Arundels and their allies politically. Later in 1387, fresh from his naval triumph, Earl Richard became one of the Lords Appellant, who challenged the chronic misgovernment of the realm and the undue influence of the King's courtiers and favourites. At the Merciless Parliament of 1388 the Appellants prevailed, having first won a military victory over Richard's principal favourite, De Vere, at Radcot Bridge. Many of the courtiers were executed – some, like Sir Simon Burley, quite unjustly. Afterwards Bishop Henry became a member of the King's Council, a position for which his loyalty to the King's person qualified him well.[20] Even so, he also appears to have been in favour of the stand taken by the Lords Appellant, who had the firm support of Bishop Thomas Arundel. If this is a correct reading of the situation, it is consistent with the part Henry played years before in the Good Parliament of 1376, where again chronic misgovernment was the issue. On that occasion he was one of the four bishops who formed part of a liaison committee between the Lords and the Commons, set up at the latter's request; and it is presumed that he was chosen not just for his youth and vigour, but because he was in favour of reform.[21]

On other occasions when he achieved prominence in Parliament the omens were far less favourable. In 1383, as we have seen, he was impeached before the Lords for his part in the failure of the Flanders Crusade, and in 1401 he was to face a situation only marginally less unpleasant. For most of the time, however, he made relatively little impression on Parliament, sometimes being named as a trier of petitions (those who vetted them before they were submitted to Parliament itself) and sometimes not. He was frequently absent from Parliament, but when he did attend he was able to fit in other tasks as well. As some at least of the other bishops were also in London there was the chance of expediting the work involved in moving clergy from one diocese to another or – increasingly – arranging exchanges under the 'choppechurches' system, which the bishops deplored, but nobody seemed able to stop. As mentioned earlier, his London headquarters was in the village of Charing, between London and Westminster, but while his temporalities were withheld, between 1383 and 1385, he had to find lodgings elsewhere. On more than one occasion he stayed with Robert Foulmere, who also had a house in the area, and during the later years of his episcopate he is sometimes found in Chelsea *(Chelcheheche juxta Westmonasterium)*, though we do not know exactly where.[22]

119

This side of his activities is, however, more than balanced by the time he spent staying in his rural manor houses, particularly Hoxne and the Elmhams, North and South. Here he could live the life of a country gentleman, well away from the distraction of national or international affairs, and close to the people who were his responsibility as father-in-God. By the standards of the time Henry seems to have been a keen letter-writer, and his letters show a warmth of personality and an engaging interest in those to whom he wrote.[23] This is refreshing when compared with some of his more eccentric characteristics.

Monuments to several of Despenser's friends and acquaintances still survive in Norfolk parish churches. Needless to say, they give little indication of what these people actually looked like, for portraiture was in its infancy, and the effigy of a knight clad in the all-enveloping bascinet and camail could hardly present distinguishing features. Perhaps the finest of these monuments is to Sir Edmund de Thorp at Ashwellthorpe, not far from Wymondham. In spite of his advanced years (he must have been approaching seventy) he went to France with Henry V and was killed in battle in 1417. His splendid alabaster tomb, which he shares with his wife Joan, is a typical product of the Derbyshire craftsmen of the time. An even more imposing, but less beautiful, monument survives at Hingham, and commemorates a younger relative of Bishop Henry, Thomas, Lord Morley, who died in 1435 and was the grandson of the other Thomas who had been a hostage of the peasants in 1381 and whom Henry knew well.

Other notables were content with a brass, or rather latten, memorial flush with the floor, with effigy, heraldry and inscriptions, as indeed Henry was himself. Among them was Sir Simon Felbrigg, standard-bearer to Richard II, who is shown with his first wife, lady-in-waiting to Queen Anne of Bohemia, in the church of that name. He did not die until 1442, but his effigy still carries his dead master's standard. When Henry IV took over, things might have gone badly for him, but fortunately he was a friend of Sir Thomas Erpingham, who saw him safely through the crisis. At Blickling is the brass of Sir Nicholas Hawberk, another fine armoured figure who was a diplomat and man of affairs until his death in 1401, while at Burnham Thorpe lies Sir William Calthorpe, the very man who did not want to be a juror and so become involved in the dispute between Bishop Henry and the burgesses of Lynn. Ancestor of a well-known Norfolk family, his fine brass is noteworthy even in a church redolent with memories of Horatio Nelson. Finally, at Reepham, one can see the mutil-ated brass of Sir William Kerdiston, a great name thereabouts, who died in 1391 and lies near his ancestor Sir Roger of 1337, whose extraordinary tomb shows him lying on a bed of sculptured stones.

But we must not forget about the people 'below stairs' who attended to the needs of the Bishop and his guests. For they strike a very discordant note. Under his esquire there was a variety of valets, pages and domestic servants. But far from the episcopal household being a model of propriety, as one might expect, it is known to have functioned, on at least two occasions, as a gang of 'heavies' offering violence, and in Edmund Clippesby's case death, to the victims they encountered.[24] What did the Bishop know about this? Certainly his esquire for the time being seems to have been the leader in these escapades, and if Henry was not aware of what was going on he should have been, and ought to have exercised closer supervision. Or is it simply the case that his household – cooks, barbers and the rest – were being permitted to behave in a way that would make the misdeeds of great men's retinues the curse of fifteenth-century England?

In spite of his affection for his manor houses, Henry's register records a second lengthy period when he hardly seems to have left Norwich at all. This extends from 11 December 1391 to 15 October 1393, with only one journey to London, in May of the latter year. Then he enters on a period of intense activity. From that day to 8 November he visits the abbey of St Benet at Holme, Bromholm Priory, Thornage, Walsingham, Creake and Lynn. Then comes another period at Norwich to 14 July 1394, broken only by a visit to North Elmham in early March, after which he begins to move around again.[25] This could lend support to a cautious diagnosis of manic depression. Even more cautious must be the conjecture that if Bishop Henry did indeed suffer from depression, his servants might have taken advantage of his mental state to go on the rampage with little fear of discipline or correction.

But matters of far greater importance were soon to engage the attention of all. The final crisis of Richard II's reign was at hand. He had never forgotten, or forgiven, those who had deprived him of favourites and courtiers in 1387 and 1388. Now, in 1397, the time had come for revenge. At the Parliament which met on 17 September of that year the Arundel brothers, together with the Duke of Gloucester and the Earl of Warwick, were accused and convicted of treason. After a vigorous and outspoken defence Earl Richard was condemned to death and beheaded. His brother, now Archbishop of Canterbury, was sentenced to perpetual banishment and forfeiture of his temporalities, while Pope Boniface IX was invited to translate him to a see effectively in the obedience of the antipope. Gloucester, having been arrested by the King in person at his castle of Pleshey in Essex, died under suspicious circumstances before he could suffer the same fate as Arundel. Warwick's death-sentence, after some abject grovelling, was commuted to perpetual banishment in the Isle of Man.[26]

This was undoubtedly a time of intense concern for the Bishop of Norwich, who was nonetheless present at that Parliament, though prudence would have dictated that he kept a low profile. Of his two friends, Richard and Thomas Arundel, one was dead and the other banished. Another friend, John, Lord Cobham, had been sent into exile in Guernsey. On the other hand his nephew, Thomas, Lord Despenser, was among Richard's victorious supporters, and was soon to be rewarded with the long-coveted earldom of Gloucester.[27] His feelings may perhaps be judged by the fact that when the second session of that Parliament began at Shrewsbury – significantly near the King's power-base in Cheshire – Henry remained in London until at least 19 February[28] when he issued a fresh commission to his vicar-general, Dr William Carleton, who had now been holding the fort for a considerable time. But he was certainly in his place at Shrewsbury on Tuesday, 18 March 1398 when, with a large concourse of bishops, abbots, nobles, lords and knights, he swore that the acts of this Parliament should be faithfully observed.[29]

But while Parliament was still in session the event that was to lead directly to Richard's deposition had already taken place. When Thomas Despenser received his earldom, five more senior peers had become dukes, though opponents scathingly referred to them as *'duketti'* – little dukes. Two of these were Thomas Mowbray, Duke of Norfolk, and Henry Bolingbroke, John of Gaunt's son, who became Duke of Hereford. The latter now revealed some compromising words Norfolk had spoken to him, to the effect that King Richard, in spite of his seeming favour, would eventually deal with them as he had already dealt with Gloucester, Warwick and the two Arundels. When taxed with this, Norfolk hotly repudiated what Hereford had said; and it was decided that the issue between the two men should be resolved through trial by battle. Elaborate preparations were made. The contestants procured the very latest armour – in Hereford's case all the way from Milan, together with Italian armourers to ensure an exact fit. But on the day of the contest, which had been fixed for Coventry on 16 September 1398, the King halted the proceedings as they were about to begin and instead sentenced both men to banishment, Hereford for ten years and Norfolk for life. Perhaps it was not in his interest that either of them should win.

From then on things went from bad to worse. Richard's conduct became more and more capricious and unbalanced.[30] Indeed, megalomania set in. So it was not surprising that when the King decided to go to Ireland to crush a rebellion there, moves to bring back Henry Bolingbroke were quickly set in train. Since the death of his father, John of Gaunt, on 3 February 1399, Henry had become Duke of Lancaster; and it was ostensibly to recover his patrimony that, counselled by Thomas Arundel, he resolved to return to England. Early in July he and a small number of followers disembarked at Ravenspur, near the mouth of the Humber.[31]

Bishop Henry's reaction was swift. On 2 July, at Bures in Suffolk, he commissioned three vicars-general instead of the usual one. John Darlington and William Carleton were joined by John, Archbishop of Smyrna, Henry's suffragan.[32] It seems as if he knew already what was afoot, and was preparing to leave his diocese for a long, perhaps an indefinite, period. This is borne out by the fact that on 10 July he was at St Albans, having raised a contingent of troops and declared for the King. This was no insignificant force, for he had at his back 62 men-at-arms and 130 archers, for whom he received government pay from the 6th to the 30th of that month.[33] Such numbers might suggest that he retained some reputation as a leader.

At St Albans he joined up with the Duke of York, whom Richard had left in charge in England. York, in common with almost all who had assembled there, was not prepared to attack Bolingbroke, he himself declaring publicly that he had been wrongfully disinherited, and that he would not oppose someone who came in a just cause to ask for the restoration of his rightful inheritance.[34] It appears, in fact, that of all the leading commanders only Bishop Henry was prepared to stand up to Bolingbroke. Viewing the fear and defeatism shown by the royal councillors he came out with a typically trenchant, if unrealistic, utterance. 'These men are doomed to die. There is no point in hoping for assistance from men who give up so easily.'[35]

Meanwhile Bolingbroke, with an ever-growing army, was approaching from the north. But London was not to be his objective for the time being. Both invaders and defenders, such as they were, moved to the westward, Bolingbroke's aim being to cut Richard off from his supporters in England when he returned from Ireland. Those supporters, apart from Bishop Henry's contingent, proved untrustworthy, and submitted to Bolingbroke at Berkeley Castle in Gloucestershire. Henry, however, steadfastly refused to submit. But resistance was useless and the result was a short period of imprisonment for him and his lieutenants. One of these was Sir William Elmham, a relative of his by marriage, one of the captains in the Flanders Crusade who had played him false, and now lord of Westhorpe in Suffolk. Clearly the two were now reconciled.[36]

The events at Berkeley, according to Higden, took place on or near 25 July, the feast of St James the Great. By 9 September Bishop Henry was far away, for on that day, at Killingworth in Northumberland, he collated John Walsingham to the benefice of Little Plumstead.[37] One can only speculate that Bolingbroke had committed him into the custody of the Earl of Northumberland or his son Harry Hotspur, and they had taken him home with them.

But however congenial his time in the north was made for him, it was a period of great difficulty and insecurity. Virtually alone, he had come out in support of his King, and the word 'stalwart' applied to him by McKisack was well earned.[38] As we have seen, loyalty for him was second nature. He would not have forgotten Richard's kindly message when he lost his temporalities in 1383, and fresh in his mind would have been the same monarch's promotion of his nephew Thomas to the earldom of Gloucester. But against that he could hardly have been unaware of Richard's marked deterioration into eccentricity, despotism and maybe mental instability. Yet at the same time he remained strongly opposed to the House of Lancaster and its representatives and supporters in East Anglia, headed by Sir Thomas Erpingham. Finally, to add to a confused situation, he had for some time been close to Archbishop Thomas Arundel, the new King's most prominent councillor.

Whatever his feelings, Bishop Henry was at his house at Charing on 29 September 1399[39], and he would have been present on the following day when Henry Bolingbroke formally claimed the crown and became King as Henry IV. He also attended the Parliament which followed from 6 October, and was one of those who agreed, surely with great reluctance, that the former King should be imprisoned.[40] He stayed on at Charing until at least 13 November, and only returned to Hoxne and his diocese on the 29th of that month, after five of the most eventful months of a more than usually eventful life.

At once he immersed himself in diocesan duties. On 2 December he was at South Elmham, instituting the new incumbent of Barrow in Suffolk, the patron of which was Sir Philip, one of the other, unrelated, family of Despensers.[41] Then, after a rapid progress around the diocese, taking in North Elmham, Thornage and Blofield, he returned to South Elmham for Christmas and remained there until the earlier part of February 1400.

It was fortunate for him that he did. For at the beginning of January the nobles who had so recently been promoted by Richard II, and had had their new dignities taken away by Henry IV, rose up in rebellion. One of them was Bishop Henry's nephew Thomas, formerly Earl of Gloucester and now again Lord Despenser. The conspirators planned to reinstate Richard, who was to be impersonated until the real Richard could be freed, by a priest called Richard Maudelyn.[42] For a short time the new King was in real danger, but with ready assistance from the citizens of London he quickly put down the rising. After attempting to escape, the leading rebels were all taken and put to death at the hands of the men of Essex, Cirencester and Bristol. It was the Bristolians who lynched Thomas Despenser. By 10 January the rebellion had been crushed.

Not unnaturally suspicion fell on Thomas' uncle. After his defiance of the new King he was bound to be a marked man. Henry himself was aware of this, for in a letter to a nephew, who must have been Sir Hugh Despenser the Younger, he protests that he was not involved in any way. He knew nothing of the rebellion until it was over, and had had no contact with the rebels, apart from a verbal message from the Earl of Huntingdon. He had never left South Elmham, except to attend the funeral of one of his servants. In conclusion he asks his nephew not to reveal this letter except in case of need, for it is best to let sleeping dogs lie.[43] But if the dogs insisted on awakening, the younger Hugh would be in a good position to speak on his uncle's behalf, for he was governor to the young Prince of Wales. Fortunately the letter does not stand by itself. Bishop Henry's register confirms that he was speaking the truth.[44]

But that was not enough. As we shall see, he had powerful enemies who had the King's ear, and Henry Despenser soon felt the weight of royal displeasure. Early in February he again commissioned vicars-general, his suffragan and the faithful John Darlington, and left the diocese once more. He is next heard of at Saltwood in Kent, where the castle belonged to the Archbishop of Canterbury. It would seem that he had been ordered into the custody of his old friend Thomas Arundel, who would be answerable for his good behaviour until the King decided otherwise.[45]

We do not know what kind of regime was imposed upon him at Saltwood, but as time went on he was usually found at Canterbury, which suggests that the restraint placed on him was very nominal. He could even transact a certain amount of diocesan business, for on 6 July he instituted new incumbents to Reymerston and Eccles, and gave Threxton to his colleague the Archbishop of Smyrna. At the same time he made John Blake Master of the Hospital of St John the Evangelist at Lynn, and commanded the Official of the Liberty of Lynn to induct him.[46] But in spite of these transactions, the bulk of the diocesan business was in the hands of the vicars-general, who from 12 July were given further help by Dr John Rickinghall, Dean of St Mary-in-the-Fields at Norwich.[47] The new commissary at once began a heavy programme of institutions. Meanwhile Henry himself instituted to Lavenham on 21 August, to the deaneries of Stow and Breckles on 8 October, and on 9 November gave the Vicarage of Thornham to John Freton, formerly Archdeacon of Norfolk and Precentor of St Mary-in-the-Fields.[48]

With the coming of 1401 the archbishop took him to London for the Parliament which met on 20 January, and while he was there he carried out two further institutions.[49] On 28 February he was back in Canterbury. But the restriction on his movements was about to be lifted, and on 27 March he was staying with Isabel, widow of the former Earl of Suffolk, at her manor of Parham. On 2 April he at last returned to South Elmham, after an absence of considerably more than a year.[50]

Even so, nominal confinement in the care of a sympathetic Archbishop had not been his only problem. His opponents had been at work undermining his position in East Anglia and seeking his destruction. At their head stood Sir Thomas Erpingham, and it is time to look a little more at the career of Bishop Henry's most determined enemy.[51]

In 1380, at the age of 22, he had entered John of Gaunt's service, and from then to the day of his death his devotion to the House of Lancaster never wavered. His antipathy to the Bishop probably began in 1383, when Despenser's 'Way of Flanders' prevailed over his master's 'Way of Spain'. He was with Gaunt in Scotland in 1385 and in Spain in 1386. By 1390 he had transferred to the service of Gaunt's son Henry Bolingbroke, going with him to fight the heathen in Prussia with the Teutonic Knights. He also accompanied him on his unsuccessful pilgrimage to the Holy Land. When his master was exiled by Richard II in 1398 Erpingham loyally went with him, and, on his return to claim his inheritance, commanded the ambush that captured the King as he made his way between the castles of Conway and Flint.[52]

But a darker side to his character now makes itself felt. On New Year's Day 1400 Erpingham was one of those who knelt before King Henry and petitioned that his predecessor be put to death. Under the circumstances this is understandable, but it is not endearing. Later, after the abortive rebellion of the 'duketti', it was he who supervised the executions of two of Richard's servants, Sir Thomas Blount and Sir Benedict Cely. They suffered the full horror of hanging, drawing and quartering, and in his agony Blount cursed Erpingham, calling him a false traitor. 'Cursed be the hour when thou and he [presumably Bolingbroke] were born.' The accusation of treachery may well be contested, bearing in mind Erpingham's long record of service to the House of Lancaster. But the editor of the chronicle that tells us this, and indeed Trevor John also, suggest that it was Erpingham's callousness and brutality (it is much too early to say sadism) that called down on him the curse of a dying man. Perhaps he could have modified the anguish of Blount and Cely had he chosen to do so; but he did not. However this may be, the Erpingham portrayed here is very different from the gallant greybeard immortalised by Shakespeare in his account of the battle of Agincourt.[53]

Others who suffered death at that time were Richard's former clerks, Richard Maudelyn – briefly Archdeacon of Sudbury – and William Ferriby. Maudelyn, who bore a close resemblance to his King, was to have been used to impersonate him, but the name of Ferriby raises the inevitable question as to whether it was the writer of Bishop Henry's register who came to this dismal end. The register itself suggests otherwise, for apart from a short passage clearly written by someone else (probably due to his illness) it is in the same hand throughout, continuing to the Bishop's death in 1406. There appear to have been at least two Ferribys, or Ferbys, active at the turn of the fourteenth and fifteenth centuries[54]and there is no indication that at this stage of his life the writer of the register extended his activites beyond the diocese of Norwich.

As for Erpingham, he made good use of the Bishop's absence at Canterbury. The balance of power had already shifted conclusively against Henry, and Sir Thomas shrewdly pressed his advantage home. In former times relations between the Bishop and the city of Norwich had been good, particularly in 1386, when the citizens enlisted him as their commander when French invasion threatened. When he visited the city in 1398, 12 shillings and four pence were spent on 'one jar of green ginger bought and given to the said lord bishop.' Perhaps he was known to like it.[55] But the citizens were anxious to win a new charter. Richard II had not obliged, and they were hopeful of a more positive response from his successor. So they made themselves agreeable to the new power in the land, offering him lavish gifts. Erpingham responded by suggesting that they would do themselves no harm if they came out against their bishop, and, taking the hint, the bailiffs and 74 of the principal citizens met together and agreed to affix the common seal of the city to charges against Henry. This can only be described as contemptible, but it worked. Norwich duly received its new charter in 1404.[56]

Erpingham also looked more closely into the Bishop's conduct at South Elmham during the rebellion of the *duketti*. The fact that he had not moved from there did not necessarily prove that he had not been plotting. He had, after all, been in touch with Huntingdon, and Erpingham made the most of it. One John Pritewell, an associate of Huntingdon, implicated Henry in his confession, but the Bishop absolutely denied his allegations.[57] He did, however, admit that he had sent for four or five local knights and esquires, and had discussed the situation with them. But far from encouraging them to rebel, he had encouraged them to remain loyal. Nevertheless, Erpingham pursued his vendetta by laying the Norwich petition before the King, together with his other charges, and asked that the Bishop should be impeached.[58]

What was his purpose in doing so? Bearing in mind what we already know about Erpingham's character, he may well have pressed for the Bishop's execution. Henry IV was quite capable of agreeing to such a request, as he showed not long afterwards when Archbishop Richard Scrope of York was beheaded. More likely, however, he was seeking imprisonment or banishment, in which case Henry, like other bishops who fell foul of authority, would have been translated to a nominal see in the jurisdiction of the antipope. For this reason, if for no other, there was something to be said for having a schism. But Henry Despenser, Bishop of Norwich, had every reason to feel uneasy as his archiepiscopal guardian took him to the Parliament that met on 20 January 1401.

127

Erpingham duly produced his accusations on Wednesday, 9 February, and was congratulated by the King for his loyalty and enthusiasm. Turning to Bishop Henry, the King taxed him with doing harm to his person through negligence or ignorance. But, he went on, in view of the Bishop's noble birth and his status as a prelate of the realm, he would be a good lord to him and extend him his favour, provided he behaved himself in the future. Archbishop Arundel then came forward and proposed that the feud should be formally laid to rest by an act of reconciliation. And so, with what feelings one can imagine, the two antagonists shook hands and exchanged the kiss of peace.[59] It is good to record that Arundel's initiative was entirely successful. There was no further trouble between them.

For Bishop Henry the outcome could hardly have been better. The King, one feels, had shown clemency because he recognised the qualities of a brave fellow-soldier, albeit an adversary. He may also have felt that Erpingham was going too far in his hostility. But another factor was of considerable, perhaps decisive, importance. For a long time Henry had cast the bread of his friendship upon the waters, and now it had come back to him.[60] Henry badly needed people to speak up for him, and many were ready and willing to do that: the Archbishop, as loyal to Henry as Henry was to him; his nephew Sir Hugh Despenser the Younger; Henry Bowet, his clerk at the time of the Flanders Crusade and about to become a bishop himself; and finally, far away in Portugal, Philippa the King's sister, now the queen of that country, who found the Bishop's kind letters and thoughtful presents a real support as she came to terms with life in a foreign land. She had been worried about the friction between her friend and her brother, and had written specially to Archbishop Arundel, asking him to use his good offices to restore peace between them.[61] Despenser's chivalry did not end with knightly accomplishments. The delicacy and charm he shows in writing to Queen Philippa show us an unsuspected and attractive side to his character.

But there was another lady to whom circumstances compelled him to write. Constance, Lady Despenser, had been left desolate by the violent death of her husband Lord Thomas; and Bishop Henry wrote her a letter of condolence and encouragement which clearly touched the heart of that great historian E. F. Jacob, and is one of the classics of medieval letter-writing.[62] I can do no better than reproduce Jacob's translation and his final comment.[63]

"'Like myself' Henry writes "who make reason sovereign over the foolishness of my flesh, you should so make your reason also: reason tells us that to watch, think, work and imagine how to recover a thing that is recoverable is well; but to grieve, sigh, languish, weep and groan over an irrecoverable thing is often the greatest folly that can be. For, first, it is great displeasure to God and a sin to murmur against his will; secondly it is a most horrible sin against nature, since by such grief a man consumes himself to death and causes himself to die"; and having sketched the disastrous results of such grief he continues: "and therefore to God, dear and sweetly loved niece, banish such folly and silliness from your heart and make reason the head of your council and your chief governor." He promises to do all he can for her honour and comfort, "for if you please, I will henceforth be to you father, uncle, husband and brother to the best of my power, and if God will, you will find this not only a fair promise, but a perfect gift." In such terms of compassionate realism, beyond all hope, but not beyond simple affection, wrote the scourge of the rebellious peasants (1381), the leader of the Flemish Crusade.'

In the months after his return to Norwich, and life returned to normal, Henry Despenser followed his own advice. No longer was he at the apex of the power structure in East Anglia. That distinction now belonged to Sir Thomas Erpingham, but the Bishop could still immerse himself in the affairs of the diocese he had been forced to leave for so long. This he did with apparent enthusiasm, and once again he and his household could be seen riding energetically through the countryside of Norfolk and Suffolk. There were, of course, unwelcome reminders of the crisis he had been through. For example, when he instituted to Stanford, near Thetford, the new incumbent was presented by the King and not by the Bishop himself, 'because the temporalities and advowsons of the said reverend father the Bishop of Norwich were recently in his (the King's) hands at the time of the vacancy in the said vicarage.'[64] This suggests that Henry again lost his temporalities when Henry IV took over the throne, but for such a short time that the escheators were not brought into action and the temporalities were not let out to farm. Perhaps the action was confined to presentations to benefices alone.

The other problem that would not go away was, of course, Lynn. A commission to various local knights and gentlemen was issued on 6 December 1401, listing the alleged misdeeds of the Bishop and his officers regarding the Mayor, aldermen and commonalty of the town, and bringing up yet again the question of the repair of Le Bysshopstathe.[65] The King's attempt to resolve the problem earlier in the year had apparently failed. Early in 1403 a much stronger commission was appointed, consisting of Henry Percy, Earl of Northumberland, Thomas Percy, Earl of Worcester, Sir Thomas Erpingham and the King's clerk Thomas Langley, later to be Bishop of Durham and

Chancellor. This was to concentrate on the long-standing dispute about the staithe, through which bishop and town had suffered heavy losses, presumably through litigation. On this occasion the town is referred to as 'the King's town and borough of Lenne', which it certainly was not. Another point of interest is that both Northumberland and Worcester were involved in the Percy conspiracy against Henry IV, which ended with the defeat of the rebels on 21 July of the same year. Worcester was executed two days later.[66] The wheel of fortune – a favourite medieval concept – sometimes revolved at a furious speed.

Other commissions and lawsuits continued the long-standing conflict, during which Bishop Henry recovered possession (seisin) of 100 acres of land and 20 acres of pasture, with damages of 1,000 marks, against John Wentworth, the Mayor, and the commonalty of that town. This happened on 11 September 1404, though an earlier writ, ordering all proceedings against the town to stop, had first to be overturned.[67] But the Bishop was not so successful when, in July 1402, he attempted to make 24 burgesses of Lynn, plus the sheriff of Norfolk, give security (mainpern) in the sum of £100 each that they would do no harm to him or to any of his servants. Between them the sheriff and the burgesses found ways of convincing the King that they had given sufficient security already, and the proceedings against them were summarily halted.[68] This pernicious dispute was to poison relationships between the bishops of Norwich and the town of Lynn for over a century to come, and gave rise to considerable violence and intimidation, particularly on the part of the townspeople.

Another source of continual, though minor, annoyance was the series of appeals made against the Bishop's disciplinary jurisdiction. For example, in 1404 (the precise day is not given) an entry in the Close Rolls records that John Talman, alias Talugman, has been excommunicated by the Bishop for contumacy. But he has appealed to the papal see and, as was the custom, to the protection of the Archbishop's court of Canterbury. Four mainpernors or sureties, John Drake, William Champeneys and John Alderforde of Norwich and John Pykynge of Norfolk, promise that they will have Talman in the chancery court in London to prosecute his appeal. Bishop Henry is required to be there also. Naturally he did not appear in person, but sending one of his legal officers to represent him involved trouble and expense even if, as is likely, he had someone in London retained to handle cases of this kind on his behalf. Several of these are recorded towards the end of his episcopate, though there is no suggestion that Lollardy was involved.[69]

Other business reaching Bishop Henry was less worrying and contentious, at least insofar as it affected him. Workman, in his usual way, imagined with what glee the old soldier would have received writs to array the clergy of

Norfolk and Suffolk for defence against enemies of the King who intended - so it was said - to invade the realm.[70] He might indeed have smiled when in May 1402 he was appointed to a commission to search out people in the same area who were telling lies about the King, to the effect that he had failed to keep the promises he made when he ascended the throne. Uneasy lay the head that had usurped a crown; and the King's common sense seems temporarily to have deserted him when he sent out such a commission.[71]

More helpfully the Bishop was required to join another commission looking into administrative malpractices,[72] while soon after he returned to his diocese from detention an order came to look into the episcopal records from the time of Edward I onwards so that the government might know the situation regarding alien priories in England. Such priories, dependent as they were on abbeys abroad, often in hostile territory, were not surprisingly regarded as security risks, and measures were taken to prevent the appointment of foreign monks as their superiors.[73] The alien priories were eventually suppressed in 1414.[74] Last of all, less than a month before he died, he was put on yet another commission charged with borrowing money in the King's name and providing adequate security to the lenders.[75] At this stage there certainly seems to have been no lack of trust between King Henry and his former antagonist. To a man of action like Bishop Henry such affairs might have seemed very pedestrian and dull; but throughout his life he had the ability to switch from important affairs of state to mundane administration in his diocese with equal contentment.

Much of Henry's correspondence comes from the last years of his life, including a letter showing that the Despensers were not immune from marital breakdown. His brother Hugh's daughter Anne had married Sir Edward Botyler, but the union was not a success. It appears that Botyler was spreading slanders about his wife; but when the Bishop tried to remonstrate with him in London he refused to see him. Now Henry writes to his friend Lady Audley asking for her help. He has begun a suit against Botyler in the court of the Archbishop of Canterbury, but he needs reliable evidence - and she can help him produce it. One of Botyler's manors - Northbery in Staffordshire - is close to Lady Audley's estates, and he asks her to send reputable people there to make enquiries. In particular, he would like to know about an old woman who is said to have died confessing that she had slandered Lady Botyler. When they have done so he would be grateful for a properly sealed deposition that could be produced in court. Miss Legge notes that the divorce Sir Edward was seeking was not granted, perhaps thanks to Bishop Henry's efforts on behalf of his niece. Fortunately there were no children of the marriage. Lady Botyler died in 1408, and her unsatisfactory husband in 1412.[76]

In medieval terms Henry was by now an old man, but there are few signs of advancing years apart, of course, from his gallstones. He administered his diocese without, apparently, needing much help from his suffragan, and his register suggests that he went to London to attend the Parliaments that met on 30 September 1402 and 14 January 1404. But he was not at Coventry later in 1404, or at the Westminster Parliament that began on 1 March 1406. From 1404 onwards he lived more and more at North Elmham, alternating when necessary with Norwich and using Gaywood occasionally when the dispute with Lynn required his attendance in that area. But he also developed a rather surprising new interest. In his last year, according to Workman, he hired rooms at Queens College, Oxford where as a very mature student he busied himself collecting versions of metrical prophecies.[77]

On 22 August 1406, at North Elmham, he conducted his final institution. Thomas Ward became incumbent of Howe, a small place near Poringland and the Framinghams to the south-east of Norwich, having exchanged with Robert Betts, who went to Herringby. Later that day he and his entourage took the familiar road to Norwich; and on the following morning, while reciting the canonical hours with his chaplains, he reached the opening words of Psalm 24: 'The earth is the Lord's, and all that therein is.' And then, quite suddenly, he died.[78]

Notes

1. For this episode see M. McKisack, *The Fourteenth Century*, Oxford, 1959, pp. 438-440.

2. He was away from Norwich between 17th July and 30th August: Register FF111R-V.

3. *Polychronicon Ranulphi Higden*, ed. J. R. Lumby, Rolls Series, 1882, vol. IX, p. 62.

4. McKisack, op. cit., p. 440 and note 1, quoting Froissart, *Chronicles*, ed. Kervyn de Lettenhove, Brussels 1870-1877, vol. X, pp. 333-339.

5. Froissart, *Chronicles*, ed. G. Brereton, Harmondsworth, 1968, pp. 303-305.

6. Ibid, p. 307.

7. *C.P.R.*, 1385-1389, p. 261.

8. Blomefield, *History of the County of Norfolk*, vol. iii, p. 112. For notes on the walls of Norwich, Great Yarmouth and Lynn see J. W. Wilton, *Earthworks and Fortifications of Norfolk*, Lowestoft, 1979, pp. 28-32.

9. *V.C.H.*, Norfolk, vol. ii, p. 485.

10. *C.CL.R.*, 1385-1389, p.169-170. One of them was John Hacoun, which in the contracted form Hacon is a Yarmouth name to this day.

11. *C.CL.R.*, 1385-1389, p. 169.

12. Froissart, ed. Brereton, p. 308.

13. See above, p.16.

14. Froissart, ed. Brereton, p. 308.

15. J. J. N. Palmer, *England, France and Christendom, 1377-1399*, London, 1972, pp. 91-93. The Flemish admiral and some 50 of his ships were captured, and another dozen or so burnt or sunk.

The account, presumably of the same action, by Walsingham is quite different. He says that the battle

132

took place of Margate, but makes the enemy fleet a combination of French and Spanish. The defences of Brest were also destroyed. Walsingham *(Historia Anglicana,* ii, p. 170) also mentions the wine!

16. Froissart, ed. K. de Lettenhove, vol. XI, p. 361 et seq.

17. Register, FF121V-122R.

18. Palmer, op. cit., pp. 93-95.

19. Walsingham, *Historia Anglicana,* ii, p. 141.

20. *D.N.B.,* XIV, pp. 410-412, quoting Froissart, XII, p. 259.

21. McKisack, op. cit., p. 389 and note 1.

22. Register, F219R.

23. M. D. Legge, (ed) *Anglo-Norman Letters and Petitions,* Oxford, 1941, passim.

24. See above, pp. 97-98.

25. Folios 161V to 192R of his register cover this period.

26. McKisack, op. cit., pp. 478-482. Politically inspired translations of senior clergy in disgrace were a feature of the period. In 1388 Alexander Neville, Archbishop of York, had been translated to St Andrews in Scotland; and at the same time Thomas Rushook of Chichester was moved to the see of Kilmore in Ireland, which was not in schism. (ibid pp. 458-459) Thomas Marke of Carlisle was translated to the see of Samothrace 'in partibus infidelium' but ended his career as an assistant bishop in the diocese of Salisbury. (E. F. Jacob, *The Fifteenth Century,* Oxford, 1961, p. 26.

27. McKisack, op. cit., p. 483. The full list was five dukes, one marquis and four earls.

28. Register, F233R.

29. *Rotuli Parliamentorum,* vol. iii, pp. 347 to 373 cover the proceedings of this Parliament.

30. McKisack, op. cit., pp. 487-491.

31. Ibid, p. 492.

32. Register, F247V.

33. Ibid. See also: *Chronicles of the Revolution 1397-1400: The Reign of Richard II,* translated and edited by C. Given-Wilson, Manchester, 1993, p. 353-4.

34. Given-Wilson, op. cit., p. 118.

35. Ibid.

36. Higden, op. cit., p. 507: *Chronique de la Traison et mort de Richart Deux d'Engleterre,* ed. B. Williams, London, 1846, Appendix, p. 292. Trevor John, 'Sir Thomas Erpingham and the Dynastic Revolution of 1399', in *Norfolk Archæology,* XXXV, p. 99.

37. Register, F248V. The willingness of John Walsingham to travel all that way after his bishop highlights the value of beneficed status. For most clergy livings were hard to come by; and every chance had to be taken whatever difficulties there might be.

38. McKisack, op. cit., p. 492.

39. Register, F249R.

40. *Rotuli Parliamentorum,* vol. iii, p. 426: 'L'Evesq de Norwiz'.

41. Register, F252V.

42. Maudelyn had been very briefly archdeacon of Sudbury: Register, FF241R and V. Thomas Hethersett then returned to his former position: F242R. I have no idea of what lay behind this.

43. Legge, op. cit., letter no. 64.

44. See Register, folios 253V to 255R for his continued residence at South Elmham.

45. Register, F256R. This is supported by the *Chronicle of Adam of Usk 1377-1421,* ed. Sir Edmund Maunde

Thompson, London, 1904, pp. 43 (Latin) and 203 (English).

46. Register, FF258R to V.

47. Register, F258V.

48. Register, FF259V, 261R, 262V.

49. Register, F264V.

50. Register, F266R.

51. See note 36 above.

52. John, op. cit., p. 96.

53. Ibid, p. 97. *Chronique de la Traison et Mort,* etc, pp. 245 (note 1) and 246.

54. *Chronicle of Adam of Usk,* pp. 42 (Latin) and 198 (English). *Chronique de la Traison et Mort,* etc, pp. 190 and note 2; 192, 196, 258 note 2, 260. See also A. B. Emden, *Biographical Register of the University of Cambridge to 1500,* Cambridge, 1963, p. 225.

55. H. B. Workman, *John Wyclif,* London, 1926, vol. ii, p. 69, quoting W. Hudson and R. C. Tingey, *Records of Norwich,* 1906, vol. ii, p. 41.

56. John, op. cit., p. 101.

57. *Chronique de la Traison et Mort,* etc, Appendix, p. 272.

58. John, op. cit., p. 101.

59. *Rotuli Parliamentorum,* iii, pp. 456-457.

60. See Ecclesiastes, chapter 11, verse 1.

61. Legge, op. cit., no. 287 (Queen Philippa to Thomas, Archbishop of Canterbury), pp. 347-348; and no. 297 (Bp Henry to Queen Philippa), p. 360.

62. Legge, op. cit., no. 62, pp. 111-112.

63. E. F. Jacob, *The Fifteenth Century,* Oxford, 1961, pp. 26-27.

64. Register, F268R.

65. *C.P.R.,* 1401-1405, p. 67.

66. *C.P.R.,* 1401-1405, p. 274: Jacob, op. cit., pp. 52-53.

67. *C.CL.R.,* 1402-1405, pp. 384, 358 (in that order).

68. *C.CL.R.,* 1399-1402, p. 575.

69. *C.CL.R.,* 1402-1405, p. 365.

70. *C.P.R.,* 1401-1405, p. 109: Workman, op. cit., ii, p. 70.

71. *C.P.R.,* 1401-1405, p. 128.

72. *C.P.R.,* 1405-1408, pp. 153-154.

73. *C.CL.R.,* 1399-1402, p. 334.

74. Jacob, op. cit., p. 300.

75. *C.P.R.,* 1405-1408, p. 200.

76. Legge, op. cit., no. 318. Her note is on p. 384.

77. Workman, op. cit., ii, pp. 69-70.

78. Ibid, p. 70.

What Manner of Man?

It remains to make a tentative assessment of Henry Despenser as a bishop, a soldier and a man.

First of all we need to put on one side judgements and prejudices that have more to do with the twentieth century than with the fourteenth. He must be judged as a man of his own time. I recall, for example, a neighbouring allotment holder who expressed interest in my studies, but when I told him that Bishop Henry had put down the Peasants' Revolt in Norfolk his reaction was immediate. 'He must have been a right old villain!' Automatically my friend applied his radical political views to an event that happened six centuries ago; and he is one of many. Then there was the time when Henry's recent successor Maurice Wood expressed reservations about the idea of unilateral nuclear disarmament. 'Bishop Despenser rides again!' proclaimed a graffito that appeared in Norwich cathedral close. Needless to say his military activities do not endear him to pacifists either, though in their case they can summon strong support from John Wyclif and the ultra-critical monk who wrote the *Eulogium Historiarum*.

In spite of the work of Canon R.A. Edwards sixty years ago Henry Despenser remains very much a bogey man, sharing the same doghouse with such as Richard III. In those circumstances the temptation to write an overtly revisionist work liberally smeared with whitewash is to be resisted. The only valid aim is to get at the truth.

What, then, can be said about Henry Despenser's military career? It is to be hoped that this study has thrown light on the unusual circumstances of his upbringing and early manhood that allowed him to move without difficulty from an ecclesiastical role to a military one and back again. Had Pope Urban V not plucked him from a career with his army in Italy and sent him to Norwich he might well have made a name for himself, as his brother Edward did, as a commander in the earlier phases of the Hundred Years War.

Brave he undoubtedly was. However great the danger he was not prepared to turn back, be it in the most dangerous phase of the Peasants' Revolt, in counselling an attack on the French army in 1383, or (virtually alone) being ready to support the king to whom he had sworn allegiance in the face of Henry Bolingbroke's successful invasion in 1399. His courage may, indeed, have led him to the verge of over-confidence if not beyond. An easy victory at North Walsham may have encouraged him to insist on leading the Flanders Crusade without any prince or leading nobleman to support him. Against that, the attack he proposed on the French army during that crusade might well have been

135

successful had most of his captains not deserted him. That army may still have been in process of formation, many who belonged to it were unused to war, and its eventual performance was indifferent to say the least. Despenser's 'few' in 1383 could well have achieved what Henry V's 'band of brothers' succeeded in doing in 1415. Apparent over-confidence and glorious victory can be the obverse and the reverse of the same coin. Luck, as Napoleon said, is crucial; and while the luck was on Bishop Henry's side in 1381 it deserted him in 1383.

But was he cruel as well as brave? Bravery, after all, is of no value if accompanied by cruelty; and Henry has often been accused of that. We must consider whether the charges stick, beginning with his conduct when he went to the aid of the beleaguered abbey of Peterborough in June 1381. Without doubt he had some of the insurgents put to death within the abbey church itself while they were seeking sanctuary. But could they really expect to be granted sanctuary when they had been caught in the act of pillage and destruction? A less hot-tempered person than Bishop Henry might have found it difficult to spare them in view of their appalling conduct.

As for the sequence of events between Peterborough and North Walsham, it seems that Henry made an example of leaders but spared the rank and file, giving them their freedom in return for a promise not to offend again. It has to be remembered that at this time he and his men were surrounded by a sea of anarchy. He could not appeal or submit to any higher authority for there was none. His only hope was to re-establish morale among the upper classes, and kid-glove methods would never succeed in doing that. But he did know the meaning of compassion for at North Walsham, having ordered Geoffrey Litster's execution and heard his confession, he supported his head so that it should not strike the ground as he was being taken to the gallows.

Turning to the Flemish Crusade the condign treatment of the defenders of Gravelines is certainly a cause for concern. According to the laws of war those who refused a direct call to surrender had to face the consequences, which were often the massacre of combatants and non-combatants alike, as Edward the Black Prince had decreed at Limoges. That was the risk they took. On the other hand a crusade, aiming to win hearts and minds to the cause of the rightful Pope, might perhaps have employed less drastic methods, for the slaughter of the defenders in such cases was by no means mandatory. In modern days Christians who disagree about doctrine or church order, would seldom dream of resorting to violence. But we are considering the fourteenth century; and in those very different circumstances the refusal of the defenders of Gravelines to surrender because they did not recognise Pope Urban may have sealed their fate rather than prompt clemency. Nevertheless Bishop Henry was in overall command, and must take responsibility for the decision.

Soon after Gravelines the Bishop and his men won a resounding victory at Dunkirk over an army sent by Louis de Mâle, Count of Flanders. Henry's enemies and detractors blamed him - and still do - for the large number of casualties his troops inflicted. Those who supported him and the crusade rejoiced at the success of English arms. In this instance, if blame is to be allocated at all, it should lie with those who committed a force so obviously inadequate, in everything but numbers, against an army equipped with archers of a high standard. One feels pity for the hapless Flemings who died, just as one does for the French who met the same fate in the same way at Crécy and Agincourt; but war has its own remorseless logic and Henry can hardly be blamed for being a victorious commander, except on the very controversial grounds that he should not have been there at all.

The greatest problem is undoubtedly Henry's involvement in the Clippesby affair. Here an unacceptable amount of special pleading is required to acquit the Bishop of blame. It was a cruel murder of an old and defenceless man, however unpleasant a character he was; and the best that can be said for Henry - if his servants did not altogether take the law into their own hands - is that anger and lack of self-control brought about consequences he deplored, while feeling obliged to be loyal to his subordinates even when they acted in a way that compromised him. He was not an even-tempered man, and Dr Rawcliffe's use of the word 'intimidating' is well merited, though it is likely that he mellowed considerably in his final years.[1]

Another comment she makes - 'probably the most colourful character to hold the see of Norwich'[2] - also appears amply justified. One gets a strong impression that Henry Despenser was a little - or more than a little - larger than life. He seems to be a man of a different stamp from the usual run of civil servants, lawyers and academics who made up the episcopacy in the later Middle Ages. Part of the colour, one might say, resides in his refusal to bow to convention and his love of doing the things he wanted to do in his own way, irrespective of the opinions of anyone else. When the French were threatening invasion in 1386 he decided that bastides were necessary to defend Flegg; so he went ahead and started to build them, entirely without authority. In legal matters he was fully prepared to take on antagonists, like St Albans Abbey, that a more prudent man would have left alone. At Lynn in 1377, admittedly early in his career, he showed conspicuous lack of judgement, made worse by supercilious aristocratic contempt, and was made to suffer for it not only on the spot but also in the pages of the greatest chronicler of the time. 'Colourful' can be an engaging attribute, but when it degenerates into irresponsibility no defence is possible.

What of Henry Despenser as a bishop? Superficial judgements have concluded that a man who was so much a soldier could not have been much of a bishop. But the reverse appears to be true. Capgrave insists that for many years he governed his people in peace, winning their hearts by a combination of generous almsgiving, warm-hearted pastoral care and a fatherly concern for the poor. At the time of the Peasants' Revolt his zeal for the protection of his flock is likened to that of the Old Testament hero Phinehas.[3] For his part Walsingham commends the firm stand he took against Lollardy and in his obituary notice stresses that his military activities were never pursued at the expense of his diocese.[4] The epitaph on his vanished brass commended him as a beloved soldier and a good shepherd.[5] Against this the monastic writer of the *Eulogium* is extremely scathing regarding his suitability for episcopal office, but his prejudice is so great that his attack may not be felt to carry much conviction.[6] One might also suggest that he would not have enjoyed Thomas Arundel's long-continued friendship had his standards as a bishop been less than worthy.

His voluminous register, though its range is restricted to institutions and not much else, reveals a competent and assiduous administrator who chose, in the main, equally competent people to work with him. He seems in return to have enjoyed their loyal support. While his attitude towards the Lollards is often held against him the fact is that in seeking to suppress them he was only acting on orders and, what is more, did so without taking a single life, his blood-curdling utterances notwithstanding. Sawtry's death cannot be laid at his door, and more extreme methods against Lollards in the diocese of Norwich did not begin until some time after his death.

After his unexplained absence from Norwich during the first two years of his episcopate his diocese saw plenty of him, in spite of necessary business in London, military interludes and periods of study at Oxford. We do not know whether this latter activity amounted to much, though towards the end of his register there are various gaps where he may have been pursuing it. Significantly he only employed a suffragan bishop towards the end of his long episcopate, and he seems never to have lost his enthusiasm for diocesan life. More than once he returned to it with redoubled vigour after unavoidable sojourns elsewhere.

There is, of course, a great deal that we do not know. Until the coming of John, Archbishop of Smyrna, did he carry out all ordinations himself? If he did not, then who did? The total absence of ordination lists in his register leaves us with no clue. More seriously, we know nothing about his spirituality. It may well have been conscientious, disciplined and chaste, but it seems unlikely that it rose much, if at all, above the conventional piety of his day. Unlike John Wyclif the status quo probably suited him well enough. Apart from belonging to the same university he and the doughty reformer had nothing whatsoever in common. But can we be altogether sure? Such an unconventional and surprising man might have had unsuspected depths and nuances in his character. What books did he own and use? Sadly his will has not survived, and one most important source of information about our medieval predecessors is therefore lost.

In his time, which was that of the Great Schism, the practice of religion in England may well have reached its lowest ebb before the conciliar movement early in the fifteenth century set about the process of reform. The rise of Lollardy is a commentary on the manifold abuses that existed, some of which – one is bound to say – can be attributed to Bishop Henry and those he employed in financing the Flanders Crusade. Strictly orthodox opinion, let alone heretics, felt that some of the fund-raising ideas employed were quite indefensible.

Not surprisingly, the majority of English people, like Henry Despenser, did not share these concerns, and saw no reason to condemn the doctrine and practice of religion with which they were so familiar. Yet even when such things are at a low ebb holiness and sanctity are bound to find their way through. In Bishop Henry's time that was certainly true. Richard Caister of St Stephen's in Norwich is a case in point. So, a little later, is Margery Kempe, the tiresome, eccentric and lachrymose holy woman from Lynn.

But most of all we see that holiness in an almost exact contemporary of the Bishop, the Lady Julian of Norwich. Did she and Henry Despenser ever meet? It is possible that he presided over the ceremony of her enclosure, whenever that was, for it called for the Bishop's attendance; but as episcopal orders were not needed to validate the ceremony one of his vicars-general may have taken his place. But if they ever communicated what might they have said to each other? Would Henry, with his pragmatic, legal mind, have been able to understand her insights? Of all the imaginary conversations one longs to reconstruct this is surely one of the most attractive. Sadly history has no time for such speculations. It only reminds us that Margery Kempe was surprisingly well received by Archbishop Arundel, even when she roundly rebuked him over the bad behaviour and foul language of his household.[7] Perhaps the warrior bishop of Norwich would have been equally considerate and humble in the presence of the Lady Julian.

He was, after all, far from being the aristocratic lout the monastic chroniclers loved to invent and then pillory. At Oxford, studying civil law, he went most of the way towards a doctorate; and he had no difficulty in recruiting, and then keeping, men of high intellectual standing to serve as diocesan officials. Moreover, in spite of his disastrous intervention at Lynn and other similar episodes, he was capable of great sensitivity, particularly as he grew older. His letters to Queen Philippa of Portugal and, most of all, to Lady Constance Despenser, show us a man who is chivalrous, affectionate, intelligent, sympathetic in a practical way and capable of abstract thought. As he writes to his nephew's widow and shows her how, even in her grief, reason needs to rule her life, one senses the very first stirrings of the Renaissance. But one is also aware of the extent to which our knowledge of Henry Despenser would have been impoverished had these letters not survived.

Early in his career Henry had gone to Italy with his brother Edward in the train of Lionel, Duke of Clarence. On Lionel's speedy demise he had stayed to fight; and it is likely that he learned to appreciate Italian art at the same time. Although he may have been one of several contributors he was probably the prime mover in the gift of the wonderful altarpiece now in St Luke's Chapel of his cathedral. This, depicting Our Lord's Passion, Crucifixion, Resurrection and Ascension was a thank-offering for the defeat of the Peasants' Revolt in 1381; and two years later it was probably Bishop Henry who gave the splendid wooden roof of the newly-completed chancel at the Great Hospital (then the Hospital of St Giles) not far away. This, furnished with sumptuous bosses and festooned with imperial eagles (though with one head rather than two) was a graceful compliment to the young Queen Anne of Bohemia, daughter of the Emperor Charles IV, when her royal husband brought her to visit Norwich and live sumptuously at the expense of its monks.

In short there are many contradictory strands in Henry Despenser's character. He could be capricious, very much an individualist, awkward, litigious, argumentative, rude and lacking in self-control. On the other hand he was loyal to a fault, a warm-hearted man who gave and received friendship freely, and a brave soldier who had the other and gentler gifts a knight was supposed to possess. Some of his conduct lends weight to the possibility that he may have been a manic depressive. As a bishop he loved his diocese, moved about it with great energy when his health permitted, and cared for its people over an exceptionally long span of thirty-six years. At the end he died in harness. He served God faithfully according to his lights, treading the path of chastity and orthodoxy to the extent that he won golden opinions in spite of his less desirable qualities.

Perhaps the clue lies in his family. While they achieved prominence, from the mid-thirteenth century to the beginning of the fifteenth, the Despensers threw up admirable characters like Hugh the Justiciar and Henry's eldest brother Edward, immortalised by Froissart. It also produced the second and third Hughs, men of a very different kind, who first brought about and then shared the ghastly fate of King Edward II. Henry, Bishop of Norwich, seems to have been an uneasy combination of the two strains. In his personality they

The roof of the chancel of the Hospital of St Giles, Norwich

fought for the mastery; but as the years went by I believe that the good progressively triumphed, so that his death was marked by genuine sorrow, widely shared.

Notes

1. Carole Rawcliffe, *The Hospitals of Medieval Norwich,* Norwich, 1995, p. 66.

2. Ibid.

3. John Capgrave, *Liber De Illustribus Henricis,* ed. F. C. Hingeston, Rolls Series, 1858, pp. 170 and 171-172. For Phinehas see Numbers 25, vv. 6-9, cf. Psalm 106, v. 30 and I Maccabees 2, v. 26.

4. Walsingham, *Historia Anglicana,* ii, p. 274.

5. Capgrave, op. cit., p. 174. To ward off criticism that a bishop should not bear arms Capgrave emphasises that Bishop Henry only fought against heretics, schismatics and disturbers of the peace.

6. *Eulogium Historiarum,* ed. F. C. Hayden, Rolls Series, vol. iii, p. 356.

7. *The Book of Margery Kempe,* edited and translated by B. A. Windeatt, Harmondsworth, 1985, pp. 71-73.

143

17, 24, 29, 77, 114, 118, 124, 129:
Despenser Retable, 50, 51, 140
Despenser, Hugh, the Justiciar, 1, 142
Despenser, Hugh the Elder, (d. 1326), 1
Despenser, Hugh the Younger, (d.1326), 1, 124, 128
Despenser, Hugh, Lord le, (d. 1349), 1, 6
Despenser, Hugh, (d.1374), 3, 4
Despenser, Hugh, (d.1401), 3
Despenser, Isabel, 5
Despenser, Joan Le, 4
Despenser, Lady Constance, 140
Despenser, Lady Elizabeth, 5, 21, 29, 41
Despenser, 26th Lord Le, 50
Despenser, Richard, 5
Despenser, Roger, 21, 29
Despenser, Sir Edward, 2
Despenser, Sir Philip, 4, 29, 30, 124
Despenser, Sir Thomas, (d. 1381), 4, 41
Despenser, Thomas, Lord le, (d. 1400), 4, 5, 29, 98,
   122, 124, 128
Dixmude, Flanders,67
Drake, John, 130
Drolle, John, 17, 96
Dublin, Ireland, 61:Deanery of, 26, 77
Duketti, 122, 126: rebellion of, 127
Dunkirk, France, 66, 67, 114, 137
Dunwich, Suff., 14: Deanery, 24
Durham, 44, 114
Durham, Bishops of, see Hatfield, Langley
Durham Cathedral, 93, 114
East Carleton, Norf., 20
East Rudham, Norf., 46
Easton, Adam, Cardinal, 94
Eccles, Norf., 125: Bishop's residence, 15, 16
Eccles, Reginald, 47
Edinburgh, Scotland, 115
Edward I, King, 1, 72
Edward II, King, 1
Edward III, King, 1, 4, 10, 13, 14, 31, 44, 72, 86
Edward IV, King, 5
Elmham, Sir William, 63, 69, 76, 123
Elsworth, Cambs., Rectory, 7
Ely, Cambs., 41, 42, 45, 118: Bps. of, 118: diocese, 22

Ely Cathedral, Cambs., 93
Erpingham, Sir Thomas, 99, 120, 124, 126, 127, 128,
   129
Essendine, Rutland, 2
Essex, 124: Peasants' Revolt, 40
Essex, Archdeaconry of, 21
Eulogium Historiarum, 60, 75, 135, 138
Evesham, battle of, 1
Ewyas, Lordship of, Herefords., 6
Exchequer, 4, 57, 59, 90, 91, 92
Eyr, Edward, 32
Fairford, Gloucs., 6
Falmouth, Viscount, 50
Faringdon, Sir William, 63, 69, 76
Fawley, Hants., 22
Felbrigg, Sir Simon, 120
Felmingham, Norf., 47
Fernes (Veurne), France, 67
Ferrers, Anne, 2: Sir Henry, 62, 76: William, Lord of
   Groby, 2
Ferriby, William, 33, 34, 126
Fersfield, Norf., 40
Fincham, Hugh, 32
Fitz Rauf, Robert, 76
Fitzalan, Richard, Earl of Arundel, 117, 119, 121, 122
FitzRalph, Richard, Archbp. of Armagh, 103
Flanders, 52, 56, 56, 57, 58, 65, 67, 73, 75, 78:
      Flanders Crusade, 6, 15, 16, 22, 24, 26, 29, 44, 48,
      58, 62, 65, 66, 68, 73, 75, 77, 78, 94, 97, 106, 108,
      114, 118, 119, 123, 126, 128, 135, 136, 137, 139:
      financing of, 59
Fleets, 118: English, 63, 65: Flemings, 118: French, 117,
   118
Flegg, Deanery, 24, 137
Flegg, East and West, Norf., 116, 117
Flemings, 34, 57, 66, 118, 137: fleet, 118
Flitcham Priory, Norf., 31
Flixton Priory, Norf., 17
Fordham, Deanery, 24
Foulmere, Robert, 22, 25, 28, 34, 59, 71, 73, 74, 76, 119
Foulsham, Norf., 23, 30
Fourth Lateran Council, 103
Fox, John, 110

148